I AM NOT MY STORY
(And Neither Are You)

Written By
ALETA MACKEY

ISBN 978-0-615-808-25-3

I dedicate this book to God—The Universe—The Divine—Love.
Without your grace and guidance, I know I would not be alive.

I dedicate this book to my children, Amber and Ginger.
You taught me to love and that I am loved.

I dedicate this book to my grandchildren, Jack, George,
Mia, Lyric, and Mathis, for showing me a love that I
did not think existed until you were placed in my heart.

I dedicate this book to my grandfather, my angel, Ken,
to my uncle and angel, Steve, and to my Aunt Kathy.
You three showed me that I am worthy of love.

And finally, I dedicate this book and the journey of writing it
to Oprah Winfrey, my soul sister, for without you sharing your
story of abuse and becoming pregnant at fourteen like myself, I
never would have started writing my story over twenty years ago.

INTRODUCTION

This is my story, told from my point of view, and based on my experiences. It is at times horrific, graphic, and raw, but it is what happened, and I will not sanitize it to make it less than what it was. I must tell my story this way for you to fully grasp what I experienced, and more importantly, to know what I survived by the grace of God. This is not designed to shock, but to help those that have been through some of the same horrors to give them hope that they, too, can make it to the other side of their trauma. I am not my story, and neither are you.

I am grateful that I don't remember the things that were worse than the horrific. There are years of my childhood that I don't remember at all. Thankfully, God spared me from those memories that I can only assume were too tragic. I believe I would have taken my own life, or slipped into some kind of psychotic state if I hadn't been given the ability to block things out. But somewhere in those years of blocked memories are moments that I do remember, and those moments have forever changed me.

In the beginning, my writing was just to set myself free. Now, my prayer is that it sets you or someone you know free. No matter what your story is, you don't have to be a victim of your past.

Please know that you are not alone!

- *Aleta Mackey*

CHAPTER 1

"Turn your wounds into wisdom."
- Oprah Winfrey

On February 22, 1967, I was born into a family of addiction, alcoholism, depression, violence, and dysfunction that spanned many generations. My father, Walter, was an alcoholic and a depressed, abusive pervert. My mother, Barbara, was described as a drug addicted, psychotic witch. My mother named me Aleta, after a Norwegian queen, and my dearly twisted father gave me my middle name, Medea, after the character in Greek Mythology who murdered her own children to spite her husband.

They were a very disturbed couple with a love-hate relationship that was based more on drugs and alcohol than love. Prior to meeting my mother, my father was in the Navy. At the request of my grandfather, former Senator Herbert Humphrey once inquired on my father's military status. A letter from the Department of the Navy followed, citing my father's trouble with both military and civil authorities, his inability to conform to military requirements, and his lack of motivation. On one occasion my father actually slashed his wrists in order to get a discharge from the Navy. Ultimately, he was discharged for attempting suicide.

Some described my mother as a witch; she wore black robes and loved tripping on acid, as well as any other recreational drugs she could get her hands on—and in the 1960's that was a lot. My father once told me that she was tripping on acid the night I was conceived.

My father was a disturbed man who created pain and trauma for others his entire life. I am unsure what happened to him as a child that caused him to be so cruel, but the fire of his madness really began to burn within his soul when his marriage to my mother came to an end. No one in my family knew who chose to divorce first, but all agreed it was a war. I was

1

only nine months old when my parents separated. My father tried to hold down several jobs, all unsuccessfully. He was never a consistent provider. There were a lot of resentments, arguments, screaming matches, and hard feelings. Unfortunately, much of that radiated out to me, even as an infant.

Bear in mind that in the 1960's it was almost impossible for a father to win sole custody of a child. It seemed an uphill battle, and it was indeed the longest child custody case in Minnesota state history, probably because it was so unheard of for a mother to lose custody of her child—until my mother's behavior made it clear that historical precedence would hold no bearing in that case. My grandfather, Kenneth Mackey, even wrote a letter regarding my mother's inability to parent.

During the divorce, I was passed back and forth between my mother and father, with neither ever having complete custody. My father was floating around, but was mostly living with my grandparents. My mother was living in a hippie commune in northern Minnesota with a man named David, and was pregnant again, which created even more resentment and estrangement with the family. My grandparents felt she was an unfit mother, so they financially supported my father in my custody battle. Truth be told, I think they were doing so in the hopes they would get to parent me themselves. I believe they recognized both my parents' inability to do so equally.

One of my earliest memories was being left in a vacant room. I was just old enough to crawl at the time and the room was bare: no furniture, just cold and dark. I remember being so scared and alone that I just found a corner and hit my head against the wall until I cried myself to sleep. Pitch-black emptiness would soon become a theme throughout my childhood. But even in that darkness, there was this little spark of light in my heart that made me know I was loved and worthy of the next breath.

At one point, my grandfather Kenneth came to visit me at the commune. My mother handed me over to him along with a diaper bag filled with dirty, waste-filled diapers. No bottles, no formula, just a bag of filth and a dirty, starved child. He was horrified at my condition and the surrounding environment. He could not stand to see me left this way, so he put me in the car and stole me back to my grandparents' home in Florida. Reports of my condition at the compound and other similar events certainly helped turn the tide in the courtroom, but the scales tipped unquestionably in my father's favor when my mother refused to seek further legal representation. She decided to represent herself, and thought it would help her case to gather up her homeless, drug addicted, and vagrant "friends" from the compound, including her new lover David (all of which had criminal records), to testify on her behalf, prove that she was a fit mother, and should be awarded custody of me. My uncle said that, in her arrogance, she made a complete ass out of herself in court, defiantly using profanity and accusing the judge of "being part of the system" of the rich versus the poor. Needless to say, she lost her case.

With her testimony and my grandparent's financial assistance for legal representation, I was awarded to my father. My mother swore revenge on all involved, and sadly enough, this included me—her own baby girl.

On November 27, 2001, I found my mother's sister and asked her to give me her side of the story regarding my parent's relationship with me at that time. The following are her words:

"Your mother was very smart; she had a high IQ and was a very needy little girl. At the age of five or so, if she felt that she wasn't getting enough attention at night, she would take her blanket and go outside to a dark place and go to sleep. It got so bad that I would open the shed door (I was only seven) so that we would know where she would be, and she would stay warm. She was an intellectual in high school with a full scholarship, but then everything changed. She met your father. Your father was an artist (unbeknownst to me), and he lived in an artist commune. Your mother was stuck on him like a magnet, and they took off to California. Our parents were livid. She then called me to tell me she was pregnant (with you) and that Walter was trying to sell some art, but she needed some clothes. I sent her some of my old maternity clothes. Soon after their place burned down, and everything—including all of your father's art and supplies—was destroyed. Sometime after that they divorced, your mother did get custody, and then your father's parents kidnapped you and took you to Florida."

"Your mother and my father hired private detectives to find you. They got a lead, packed up, went to Florida, and knocked on the door. Your mother was then arrested for vagrancy. While in jail, your mother had an embolism and almost died. In fact, she was pronounced dead during surgery. Somehow she came back, but we believe that her mental capacity had been altered."

After speaking with my aunt, I knew that each side of the family had their own story, and my mother had certainly told her family the story in her favor. But regardless of who says who did what, the atrocities that were done to me as a child were unspeakable, and I wished they never happened. Thank God that I had a few core people in my life to sustain me.

These were the people that I remember from my childhood as my angels: my father's parents, Grandpa Ken and Grandma Olza; my father's brother, Uncle Steve, and his wife Aunt Kathy. They loved me, which is really what I needed most... what every child needs most. Looking back, their love was the energy and the oxygen that kept me alive.

"We do not come to believe in ourselves until someone reveals that deep inside, something is valuable, worth listening to, worthy of our trust, sacred to our touch, spirit comes alive when we are made alive by LOVE."

This was written for me when I was a child by my Aunt, Kathy Mackey.

CHAPTER 2

"Nothing ever happened in the past that can prevent you from being present now; and if the past cannot prevent you from being present now, what power does it have?"
- Eckhart Tolle

One vivid memory from my childhood happened during one of my mother's visitation weekends. I ran to the door when she knocked, pulled a chair underneath the knob, and put the chain on the door.

"Grandpa, please don't make me go with her. She's mean!" I cried.

Heartbreak permeated from his eyes. He did not want to let me go. He wanted to hold me in his arms and protect me from her and any other pain I might endure at her hand. I was his little angel and he was my guardian. Little did he know that it was the last he and grandma would see of me for a very long time. I was only three years old.

My mother kidnapped me and took me to Mexico. She was a drug dealer, smuggling large amounts of heroin across the border in her station wagon, under the guise of a loving mother with her beautiful blonde-haired, blue-eyed daughter in the back seat.

The shack we lived in smelled of poverty, darkness, and pain. My sleeping quarter was a wire chicken cage with a padlock on the door on the outside of the shack against the wall. I was left without food and water while the bugs fed on me. Roaches scurried at my feet and mosquitoes drained me of the little fluid left in my body. I was so dehydrated and so very scared. My tongue felt like a dried sponge, and the hunger pains were so intense that I felt that my stomach was eating itself. My ribs were crumbling inside of me. I had no sense of time, only the awareness of day and night. I would cry to my mother from the cage, begging her for food, water, and of course, love. I didn't understand...I couldn't understand what I had done to make her do this to me.

"Please, mommy! I love you, I won't be bad."

This was the start of my definition of "not good enough." I felt like I must be perfect or I would get tortured. That feeling has lingered with me to this day. At times I still have to remind myself that it's okay if I leave a dirty dish in the sink, and that no one will choke me, rape me, burn me, or hurt me.

With hatred in her eyes that matched the glowing embers of her cigarette, she would burn me with cigarettes to shut me up when I cried. My screams drowned out the sizzling sounds. That memory did not come up until I was sixteen years old during my first medical exam. The doctor questioned me about all of the burn spots on my body that were circular—the circumference of a cigarette—and one large one on my shoulder that was hidden by the immunization site. Later that night, it all came flooding back. It was one more horrific memory I'd buried deep within, only to surface when I could mentally handle it.

I cried alone at night in my cage, *"Please, God, send me an angel to save me! Set me free! Take me to a place where someone will hold me, feed me, and let me know they are not going to leave me alone. What have I done to deserve this? What have I done? Help me sun, help me moon, help me stars, help me anyone. Grandpa, where are you?"*

The only fond memory I have of Mexico is making my mom's drug runs with her and being able to get hot bread on the way. The smell of hot bread gave me such comfort. The taste of the bread made me feel warm inside. To this day, warm bread with butter makes me melt inside. I am not sure how long I was in that cage before we left for Canada, the next stop on my mother's fugitive path. Maybe weeks...maybe months. Time is often not a part of the life of children who are being abused. Not in my case, anyway. My memories and concept of time are very fragmented.

CHAPTER 3

*"I am highly allergic to people treating
me with disrespect, including myself!"*
- Aleta Mackey

Finally, I was freed from the cage in Mexico, only to find that we were on the run once again, this time to Canada. I remember being surrounded by the most beautiful leaves I had ever seen. I was set free to be outside with Mother Nature—no cage, no bugs, and there was food. The colors of the leaves were so vivid that I felt I was in Heaven. I will never know what changed in her mind to set me free, but I was grateful.

It was a whole new world away from the harsh reality of the cage. The trees and leaves were so beautiful there! If I could have crawled under a pile of those leaves and melted into the depths of the soil, I would have. Maybe Mother Earth would want me as her child.

Once in Canada, my mother's lover, David, joined us again. But this would offer me no comfort, and neither would he. He was just someone else that took away the attention and love that I so desperately wanted from my mother.

I was maybe four years old when I remember being woken one night by the sound of my mother crying. Strange that after all she had put me through that I would even care or have any instinct to protect her from whatever may be hurting her. I ran into the next room just in time to see my half sister's head pop out of my mother's vagina. This was such a disgusting, painful experience for me. I was too young to understand the blood, the screaming, and the cutting of the cord. I do remember feeling this dark twinge of excitement when my mother screamed in pain. I smiled inside and thought, *"Now you know how it feels to hurt."* The dark passenger in my mind tried to raise its ugly head and take over, but somehow I knew that if I "believed," the light would always cast it away.

After my half-sister's birth, my mother dumped her off onto me while she and David left. I became the babysitter. Again, I was not even five years old, but I was given the responsibility of the new baby when in fact I needed a babysitter myself. I was far too young to be left alone by myself, let alone left with a baby. It became even harder for me when she began crawling. She was getting into everything, and I didn't know how to take care of her. I didn't even know how to take care of myself!

Once, I left the room for just a moment, and when I came back she was bleeding from her mouth. She had somehow gotten into the trash or something and was eating glass. I was screaming for help but realized once again that I was alone. I didn't know what to do so I washed her mouth out. No one was there for us. I thought she was going to die and that it was my fault.

There can be no more accurate definition of Hell for a child than abandonment. A child's very life is giving and receiving love. To be deprived of this is death, and indeed I felt I was dying inside. But I clung to the hope that someday life would be beautiful, even though at this point I had no reason to. I believed life could be loving and safe "somewhere." I held my heart open to the vision of a place for me to love and be loved in return. That is the natural instinct of any child with a normal childhood, but for me, the battered, the dead, it would be a miracle. The feeling of that special Heaven resonated deep within my soul...it was my only lifeline, and it was the key to keeping me alive.

CHAPTER 4

"There is no greater agony than bearing an untold story inside you."
-Maya Angelou

Soon we were on the move again. I can only guess that it was because my mother was running from the law. This time it was to Oregon, and we moved into another hippie commune in Eugene. It was more like a cult compound, actually. One night, mom had a bunch of people over for one of her "parties"—which usually turned into drug-induced orgies—and this one was no different. At the tender age of five, my mother left me right in the middle of it.

Everyone around me was having sex. At the time I didn't know what they were doing. I do know that I was scared. What may have been sounds of pleasure to an adult were nightmarish screams of pain from people who did not even seem human to me, especially in their chemically-induced, semi-psychotic state. I didn't even know where my mother was in this twisted Bacchanal scene. Picture a five-year-old child looking for their mommy in this frenzy of flesh. I was scared to death. I hid at the bottom of my sleeping bag, shaking with fear that someone would find me. And my worst fears were realized. Someone did.

I can only guess what amount of narcotic or psychedelic drugs would allow a man to do to a child what he did to me. I have blocked the pain of having a full-sized penis going inside of my child-sized vagina. I do know that I was never a child again. I lost my power and my innocence to that man. I was murdered.

For many years I hated him for stealing that from me. I couldn't tell anyone what had happened. I was too young to even understand it, much less articulate it. This horrific memory was so well blocked that it took many years of therapy as an adult to bring it back to the surface to be healed.

9

I was very sexually stimulated after that event. I am unsure why this happens to some sexually abused children, especially when the event was so incredibly painful. It would seem to me that if someone hurt me that bad, I would become repulsed by sex, but it made me want more. I believe that my mind thought sex was love, the thing I was starved for more than food or water. Love was what I craved, and as sad and twisted as it was, this tragic event was the closest thing I could find to love. It was the most attention I had gotten from any adult, including my mother, since she kidnapped me. All I had ever wanted was to be loved. My body and soul ached for any affection, any validation that I was worthy, that I was enough. Even hugs were like a drink of water in the desert for me.

It was soon after that incident that my mother was arrested in El Paso, Texas and jailed for smuggling heroin over the Mexican border. She left me at the compound in Oregon with my keepers, in the "community" which likely included my offender. She was also wanted for credit card fraud and for kidnapping me. To avoid extradition to Minnesota, she plea-bargained in exchange for telling the authorities where I was. The detectives told my father and grandparents where to find me. My father flew out and rescued me from the compound with the help of the local police. He was my hero, my daddy. My perfect, loving daddy.

When they found me, I was covered with burn scars from cigarettes, and I was drugged. My mom and the others had been giving me marijuana tea and butter hash brownies to keep me quiet and easy to care for. I was sexually stimulated and aware at five years old. Whether they put two and two together about the sexual abuse that caused it, I do not know. But finally, I was rescued. I was free from this demon posing as my mother. I was safe from harm, at least by her hand.

I was returned to the safety of my father, my hero's arms. Soon I would discover that safety with him was also an illusion, but for now I felt safe and loved. We flew from Oregon to my grandparent's home in Altamonte Springs, Florida, where we would stay.

My grandparents were so happy to see me. A few days later they actually had a party…for me! Many people were there, celebrating my return to my grandparent's arms after over two years of being abducted by my mother. There was so much joy and celebration! For one of the first times in my few years of existence, I felt loved and valued. They were actually celebrating **me**! My heart felt full; I could breathe.

Grandpa put me to bed in his big bed that night. He did not want me to sleep alone after all I had been through. He tucked me in, kissed me good night, and with a tear in his eye, he told me he loved me and gave me the most beautiful hug. Now before you wonder, it was NOT a sexual thing. The sexual stimulation that I spoke of earlier was not a factor there. That attraction to false affection fell away in the presence of real love. Grandpa was the only one who made me feel like a real kid, a normal little kid, and I felt his love fill my heart. I was home.

Later that night, as I lay in bed listening to all of the adults laugh and talk, I suddenly heard a scream. It was my grandma, and I was paralyzed with fear at what could have made her scream that way. I couldn't move. I was waiting, praying for my grandpa to come tell me everything was okay. Then I heard a siren approaching the house. I couldn't take it anymore, so I jumped from my bed and ran to the window just in time to see my grandpa being wheeled out on a stretcher. And just like that, my angel was gone. I never saw my grandpa again.

He had died of a heart attack.

CHAPTER 5

"True forgiveness is when you can say,
'Thank you for that experience.'"
- Oprah Winfrey

I think my grandpa had to know that his little angel was safe before he could leave this life...he had waited for me! In truth, I believe he was my angel, my savior. It was because of the true love that he showed me that I was able to know that love existed and was available to me, no matter what I had suffered or what suffering was still to come. The unconditional love he shared with me allowed me to set my compass to a better life.

I remember the times when I lived with Grandpa, during the divorce proceedings and for the few days after my rescue, as some of the happiest in my life. He would come home from work and grab me up with the most lovable hug, like he was seeing me for the first time ever. I don't remember who said this originally, but Oprah mentioned this: "That a child should see your face light up when they enter the room, this is how they know they are valued and loved." I felt this with my grandpa. He would sit me on his lap, bounce me on his knee, and he would always have candy in his pocket for me. Those little pieces of chocolate seemed to be filled with love.

Whenever I would get upset over anything, I would stick my bottom lip out in the most comical pout.

He would say, *"Tita, the blue bird of happiness is coming. I see it now. See? Look out the window. I hear it... here it comes..."*

I would play along and say, *"I see it grandpa! What is it going to do?"*

He would smile and say, *"It's going to come poop on your lip!"*

I would giggle and that pout would vanish and be replaced by joy.

Grandpa could always make me laugh. He did not want me to feel any pain. He knew I had already suffered more pain than any child should ever have to endure. Happiness and innocence were restored when I was with my grandpa. When I lost a tooth, he put silver dollars under my pillow. He thought he was being quiet when he came in as the tooth fairy, but I never slept soundly like normal children. I was always aware of my surroundings, fearful that some stranger might sneak into my room to rob me of my innocence once again.

I remember I loved wearing cowboy boots with dresses, and grandpa would let me. He accepted me, just as I was. He let me be a little girl again, running around in my goofy outfits, my blonde hair and big blue eyes twinkling in the sunshine.

I loved to swim in the pool at grandpa and grandma's house. The combination of the warmth of the sun and the water somehow felt like a safe place to me. This was a place where I could go and float my worries away. I remember grandpa got me a tiny sailboat that I would play with in the pool for hours.

My grandparents told me that I had a love for water since I started walking. They said I would open the screen door, go to the pool, take off my diaper, and sit on the top step in the pool and wade my feet. They were always watching me very carefully, just not where I could see them. I would then get out of the pool, put my diaper back on and sneak back in the house. They were always there to protect me, but still allowed me to discover things and express myself.

This relationship between my grandfather and I was the first real love I had ever felt in my life. He truly was and is my angel. And then, after his death, he was gone. I was shattered. The security and stability that I had regained started to crumble around me.

After grandpa's death, I turned to my dad for love and comfort. But once he had rescued me, he found caring for me was more responsibility than he was willing to accept, so he handed me off to my grandma and disappeared, again. This was his pattern: a brief, half-hearted attempt to take care of me, and then hand me off to either my grandparents or my aunt and uncle. They loved and cared for me as their own, and just when I would start to feel stable and normal again, he would reappear, say that he was ready to be a father, and demand they give me back.

The two most important people in a child's life are their mother and father. Mine either abused me or disposed of me like yesterday's newspaper. You can only imagine the damage this does to a child's confidence...to my confidence, as well as my self worth, heart, and mind. It was devastating. I felt that no one in my life could or would love me for very long. I felt that I was not worthy of being loved, or of being in any stable environment. I developed a deep-seeded belief that I was NOT GOOD ENOUGH. That has affected me my whole life. But I'm jumping ahead a little.

My father left me with my mourning grandmother and took off to who-knows-where. The day my grandpa died, my grandmother died too. Not in body, but in mind and spirit. Grandma's marriage with grandpa lasted over thirty years. They loved each other very much, and she was completely intertwined and enmeshed with him, so much so that she didn't know how to live without him. In fact, she didn't want to. She made it known after his death that she was ready to die as well, and her actions made that perfectly clear. She began chain smoking, drinking heavily, and became completely dependent upon alcohol.

I think she was too afraid to commit suicide outright. She was probably in denial that she was doing so by poisoning her body with alcohol. With the loss of her beloved Kenneth, she had simply lost the will to live. She consumed the maximum amount of alcohol that she physically could, everyday. She became a drunk. For a year, the family was unaware of how severe it had become, and unfortunately that was during the time my father had left me alone in her care. Sadly, it was the other way around.

I would have to fend for myself when grandma drank, which was constantly. Even at five to six years old, that was something I was used to doing. Whenever I could, I would go to the pool, my safe place, to escape her path of destruction.

We would go out to eat often, or in her case out to drink, and she would get so drunk that she would start fights with the waiters and restaurant managers. She would complain about the food and start screaming and yelling at them in an attempt to get free food (which she never ate anyway) and drinks. I was so embarrassed and humiliated. I wanted to hide under the table.

She would then attempt to find her way home driving drunk, usually got lost, and often drove half the speed limit on the highway and double the speed limit through residential areas. When she would get pulled over, the police would just reprimand her and escort us home. Laws were different then.

One night, as I was sleeping, I awoke to a loud crashing noise in the living room. I peeked out the door and there was grandma, lying unconscious in a bloody pile of broken glass that used to be the coffee table. She had been drinking again and fell through the glass table during one of her blackouts. Another time, she fell in the shower, and another still, she fell through the patio sliding glass door. Luckily, none of her injuries were fatal, but I doubt she shared my views of that being good fortune.

On another occasion, I came home from school to find her passed out drunk under the kitchen table. She was naked and had shit all over herself. That was more than I could handle. I had no idea what to do with her anymore. I ran out of the house and sat under a tree with my head in my hands, crying and praying:

"God, please send my dad to come and pick me up! Anyone, please get me out of here! Grandma scares me so much! I don't know what to do!"

Suddenly, I felt warmth in my heart and the touch of an angel near my shoulder. It felt familiar, and I knew it was my Grandpa Ken. A sense of peace came over me that told me tomorrow would be a better day. I was given reassurance to not worry during any day with pain, because tomorrow would always be a better day. I rested under that tree in peace until late that night, after grandma had woken and cleaned herself up.

I called my Uncle Steve to come save me many times that year. I would tell him of my grandma's tragic escapades, and that I was scared of her and didn't know what to do. I'm not sure which event was the deciding factor for him, but he finally realized that she was beyond the point of no return, and that I was in danger, so he came to get me.

Grandma was put in a nursing home, and I moved in with my Uncle Steve, Aunt Kathy, and their newborn son, Ryan, for the next two years. Steve and Kathy were a normal, loving couple. They gave me love and stability by raising me as their own. I started to feel like a normal kid again. You may remember this scenario from earlier when I said I was jumping ahead. If you do, you know what is coming next. That's right, my dad suddenly reappeared and demanded his child, saying he was ready to be a father again.

Admittedly, I had mixed emotions. On one hand, I didn't want to leave Steve and Kathy because I loved them dearly and they loved me.

On the other, he was my Daddy. He actually wanted me and wanted to love me like I had always wanted him to do. The archetypes of mother and father are the archetypes for God to a child, and the source of their identity and fulfillment. So I was happy to be with my father again, to have a chance at healing wounds too long left open.

CHAPTER 6

"One of the hardest things in life to learn is which
bridges to cross and which bridges to burn."
- Oprah Winfrey

After my dad collected me from Steve and Kathy's, he said we were moving from Florida to Colorado. During the road trip to Colorado with my dad, I felt safe as I lay in his lap, looking at the odometer turn and gazing at the moon above. I wondered how the moon kept following me wherever I went. Maybe it was another one of my protectors of light, like grandpa. It seemed that she (the moon) was always there for me and I felt safe.

At that time, my dad was still God in my eyes. He had not hurt me, and I justified him abandoning me as often as he did. I just thought he had a job that made him leave a lot. It's funny how a child will create stories to keep their parents in good standing. I trusted him and felt safe and loved by him.

Once in Colorado, we moved into a motel with a dirty bar, pool tables, pinball machines, and rough, drunk, and dirty men. We were in coal mining country, and that is where we would stay for the next three months. We shared a bed in a small, dingy room that was just down the hall from the bar. Dad got a job as a coal miner and enrolled me at the local school. At first things were good; I was just so happy to be with him. We would have hamburgers and play rock, paper, scissors. Whoever lost would get a swat across the wrist. I was strong; I was not going to be a sissy girl. I was going to show him that I could handle pain, which I could. And honestly, I wanted his attention so desperately that it would not have mattered if he was flogging me.

I attended school while he worked in the mines, and I am amazed at the little things that I remember that seemed so simple, yet would affect my life in the future. A dental hygienist gave us these little tablets that we chewed up to show us where we missed brushing our teeth. It showed the plaque in pink. That was the tool she used to show us the importance of taking the time to brush our teeth. I remember that event so vividly, and how interesting teeth were. Later in my life you will see how these seemingly small details eventually came full circle.

Every night when my dad returned to our seedy motel room from the mines, we would go straight to that dirty bar. I would play pool and pinball while dad sat and drank. The darkness in him grew larger, and became more and more dominant. I was eight years old then, and had become quite the pool shark and pinball wizard. I tried to acquire whatever skill I could to impress my dad in that seedy world he chose for us, but no pool or pinball trick could suppress the beast that was rising in him and the abuse that was soon to follow.

Every time he drank he became angry, dark, and evil. He was not my father anymore, and I became afraid of him. It was almost as though he became a separate entity altogether, and became more and more attached to that bar. I would come to him for attention, hoping to get it from my daddy, not the drunk, dark one. He would just hand me a handful of quarters and tell me to go play pool or pinball. Hardly an ideal home or family life for an eight-year-old child, but I didn't complain. I was happy to get any attention from him, and often just desired to be in the same room. Soon I would get more attention than I ever wanted.

CHAPTER 7

*"Life will give you whatever experience is most helpful
for the evolution of your consciousness. How do you
know this is the experience you need? Because this
is the experience you are having at this moment."*
– Eckhart Tolle

One night, like so many before, we got back to our room and I put my pajamas on as usual and got into bed. Dad was completely wasted, and I was not even sure he was conscious as I said, *"Goodnight, Daddy,"* and went to give him a hug. But something in him was awake, and when I hugged him, he wouldn't let go. He started pawing at me, clumsily trying to pull my pajamas off. I tried to push him off me, but I was no match for his strength. When I looked in his eyes, I didn't recognize what was looking back at me.

I wanted to say, *"Daddy, please stop!"* but I was paralyzed with fear.

That was not my father. He pinned me down and pulled my pajama bottoms off as I lay there in terror of him, terror of what was to come. Next, he removed my innocence, what little was left. I had experienced someone forcing sex on me before, but that time it was my dad.

I lay there motionless, tears streaming down my cheeks, hoping somehow that it would go away. He slowly spread my legs apart.

"Daddy, no…"

He went down on me, forcing his tongue in my tiny vagina, rubbing his rough beard between my legs. I tried to leave my body, unable to handle what was happening. Shocked, sickened, and unable to leave fast enough, I suddenly threw up all over him. Enraged, he looked up at me with a growl, and I swear the beast I saw in his eyes was Satan himself. I was terrified and traumatized, and realized that I must clean it up immediately to escape further punishment.

"I'm sorry, Daddy. I'm sorry," I cried.

From that moment on, he was no longer my daddy, and I could never be his little girl again. Tita, that sweet little girl that I once was, the one that was rescued by Grandpa, was gone. I was forced to become Aleta, a woman in a child's body with a closed heart, with no ability to trust anyone or accept that anyone would ever love me for me, just me, for a very long time.

I know now that his actions were done by a sick, perverted man who was seriously disturbed and that it was not my fault. That was not love. I was only eight years old! By day he was a coal miner, by night he was a pedophile. I knew that I could not tell a soul about what he did to me. I knew he would kill me.

I tried to go to school the next day and pretend none of it had ever happened, but I couldn't. I was scared beyond the ability to mask it with a fragile smile. I was withdrawn and distant. When teachers asked me if I was okay or if something was wrong, something came out of my mouth to cover or explain my shattered state, but I don't know what it was. I only heard it as a faint echo from the bottom of my deep pit of despair. I would tell them anything they wanted to hear to get them to leave me alone, anything but the truth.

The truth was something I couldn't even stand to hear or consider myself. People can sustain serious injuries, even dismemberment, and carry on as long as they don't know how badly they're hurt. It's when they're forced to look at the injury and the reality of its severity that all of the pain comes rushing in and they collapse, unable to carry on. The same is true of emotional trauma. The same was true for me.

On the playground, I would hang from my feet on the monkey bars and let all the blood drain to my head. I would look at all the other children laughing and wonder how it felt to go home to their house instead of my dirty motel room. I remember just letting go and falling flat down onto a rock in the middle of my back and being unable to breathe. I just lied there in shock, with the breath knocked out of me, unable to shed a single tear. I looked up at my teacher who had come running over.

She said, *"Let's call your parents."*

Silently, I said to myself, *"I don't have any that care enough to come and rescue me. Please just let me lay here and die."*

Suddenly I understood grandma's suicidal drive, and how the pain was just too much to bear. My teacher ended up driving me to the motel on her own. When we arrived, I could see the look on her face. The pity. I looked to her in shame and with feint hope that she would do something.

"Help me, please…" I whispered in my mind.

She did nothing. Not one person in my life saved me during the years of my child abuse. No parent, teacher, neighbor, not anyone. Not one person spoke up. Why do people turn a blind eye on a child that is obviously in a harmful and painful home life?

CHAPTER 8

"The first time someone shows you who they are, believe them."
- Maya Angelou

Soon after my incestuous violation, my dad found another woman, the kind of quality companion that one could expect to find in a seedy motel bar in a coal-mining town. I suppose she offered him things that an eight-year-old girl could not. He started paying more attention to this woman, and I became yesterday's news once again. As sick as it was, that "love" from daddy was all I knew. It was all I had.

Like a jealous girlfriend, I let it be known that I did not want her around with my brat-like behavior. I clearly remember sitting on the bench outside the motel with my father on one side of me and his new toy on the other, and saying something very smart-ass. What I was really saying was *"Please love me more! Don't leave me for her!"* But I'm sure it was lost in translation. He turned and slapped me across the face with enough force to knock over a full-grown man. Getting slapped so hard by my father in the cold of winter was a sting that felt like a two-by-four across glass that shattered my face and my heart.

I was so embarrassed and hurt that I ran. I ran and hid underneath a nearby bridge. I sat shivering and crying next to the frozen water of the stream. I sat there waiting for my father to come find me, rescue me, and apologize, or at least try to ease my pain. I just needed him to show me he cared in some small way. He never came, and my heart froze colder than the water ever could.

I knew that if I stayed there any longer I would quickly freeze to death. I was forced into a walk of shame, my tears still frozen to my face, along with the trickle of blood still frozen under my nostril from the slap. I went back to the bar, past the pool tables, past the drunken men, past the pinball machine, and down the dark hall to the room we shared that still held a hint of vomit and reeked of pain and shame from my father's incestuous act so many nights ago.

When I tried to open the door, it was locked. With salt in the wound, I then had to knock like some stranger, not like a daughter. My father opened the door and just stared at me for a moment without letting me in. I stared up at him, my eyes begging for some breadcrumb of affection or forgiveness. Finally, he spoke without emotion or concern, simply handed me a ten-dollar bill, and told me to go to the bar and get him some cigarettes. Then he instructed me to clean up while I was there because I 'looked like a fucking mess.'

CHAPTER 9

"If a man wants you, nothing can keep him away.
If he doesn't want you, nothing can make him stay."
- Oprah Winfrey

Soon we left the coal-mining town, left the seedy motel, and left my innocence in the room where it was taken. We did not stay anywhere for long periods of time after that, and I was never in a school for longer than three months. I had no chance to make friends and no chance to grow any roots, because anytime I started to, I was ripped out of the ground again and put into another strange environment, made to start over. That in itself gave me major insecurities, let alone the burden of the shame I was carrying. I would listen to the other kids talking about their great family lives:

"My *daddy took me to the movies.*"

"*Well,* my *daddy took me to the zoo.*"

All I could think of when I wanted to speak was, "*My daddy took... me.*"

In order to be able to speak at all, and in the hopes of fitting in, I developed the ability to become an incredible dreamer-liar. I became so eloquent with my stories of a beautiful home life, of how my father was so important and how we traveled all the time, even to exotic locations, of how much he loved me...that I began to believe it myself. I was swept away in my wonderful fantasy world, until I went home and saw the hell I actually lived in.

I remember we ended up on a ranch in Minnesota at one point. My father put me to work tending to the horses. I mostly mucked out the stalls, but I also got to brush their beautiful hair sometimes too. We had an apartment above the training arena in the barn area. When my dad wasn't around, the other handlers let me ride the horses. I loved the horses. I felt that somehow they sensed my pain and were tender and nurturing with me. I had such a connection with them. I loved the majestic beauty of horses, and when we left I missed having them in my life.

I can recall a few painful memories from the time at the ranch, besides my father's continuing emotional abuse and neglect. One memory was of getting kicked by a horse. I don't blame the horse, I was just in the wrong place at the wrong time and I spooked him. Having never been around horses before, I didn't know that you don't walk up behind a horse without establishing your presence and purpose first. He kicked me in the chest and sent me flying across the barn. Luckily, I was not hurt too badly, just shocked, bruised, and had the wind knocked out of me. As expected, when dad saw it, rather than running to see if I was okay, he just looked at me with shame and disapproval and went back to work.

I once rescued a baby bird that fell from its nest. I attempted to feed it and nurture it, but it did not live. I felt so guilty, like it was my fault. That event further fed my belief that I was not good enough or able to have and share love.

The owners of the ranch had two giant poodles that attacked me once. They say that dogs can smell fear, and have an instinct dating back to the wolves to eliminate the smallest and weakest in the pack. When the handlers were not around, the hounds seized their opportunity and closed in for the kill. As an eight year old, these dogs stood to my shoulder, easily able to overpower me, so they may as well have been wolves. I was terrified. I ran as fast as I could, knowing that my life depended on it. I screamed, but there was no one around. The closest thing to shelter or safety was a car that was close by. I leapt for the car, the dogs snapping at my heels as I crested the roof.

Eventually they got bored with terrorizing me and realized there was probably easier food elsewhere, so they left. I ran home as fast as I could, not saying a word to my father, knowing it would somehow be my fault and deserving of more punishment.

One of my father's jobs was to take big trash bags full of sawdust and woodchips that were delivered to the ranch and empty them into the bottom of the stalls for the horses. These bags were stored in the barn and stacked against the wall, creating a forty-five degree angle almost to the top of the barn. On the opposite wall of the barn, hay bales were stacked high in the same fashion, and in the middle there was a wonderful rope swing that hung from the upper deck that the owners had set up for their kids to play on when they were around.

The hay bales were okay to climb on, however I was not supposed to play on or near the bags of woodchips in case I broke or tore them, which would add to my father's workload, and subsequently my punishments. But the angle of that rope swing made them an irresistible landing pad. I would go and play in the barn when he wasn't around and swing off the rope on the upper deck and land on the bags below, often tearing them in the process. I didn't care. I was so angry with my father for what he had done to me, as well as his lack of love, and that was one of the only ways I could think of to affect him and make him suffer in return. I would run up the bags, tearing holes in them the size of my foot, then jump up to the rope to swing again.

He would get so angry when he found the torn bags and ask me if I had been playing in the barn. I would always lie and say no. I don't think he believed me, but he never punished me for it without knowing for sure, which was kind of strange that he spared me based on some sense of logic or justice that had been absent every other time. So I continued my subversive acts of treason, and I went to play in the barn again after he was gone. I climbed to the top deck to swing from the rope onto the bags below, but I lost my grip on the rope and fell fifteen feet to the hard floor of the barn. I landed on my left knee with all of my weight and cracked my patella. I was in agony, but I knew it would pale in comparison to the pain I had coming if I confessed my crime.

I limped home the best I could and tried to act like nothing was wrong. I was terrified to tell him, but soon my knee began to swell and the pain became unbearable. I was finally forced to timidly tell him that I fell from the rope swing, knowing that it implicated me in the tearing of the bags. He knew he had me, and refused to do anything about my knee until I admitted to his suspicions.

"But, Daddy, it hurts!" I cried.

Those words had meant nothing to him before; I don't know why I thought they would matter that day.

As my knee continued to swell and bruise, I finally gave in and admitted my transgression. He looked at me with hatred in his eyes and said:

"I'm going to take you to the hospital…and you'd better hope

something is broken or I'm going to break something when we get back."

We drove to the ER without saying a word, just me trying to choke back my sobs. The x-ray revealed a broken bone, which resulted in a cast on my leg. On the ride home and in the days that followed, his silence and anger remained, making the distance between us even greater. In some ways I think I might have preferred the beating…

One of the most painful memories of that time was getting and losing my first puppy. A beautiful pudgy German Sheppard "disappeared" off our front porch, just when I began to open my heart to loving something. It took me years and several more animal tragedies to allow myself to love an animal again.

CHAPTER 10

"Dogs are my favorite role models. I want to work like a dog, doing
what I was born to do with joy and purpose. I want to play like a dog,
with total, jolly abandon. I want to love like a dog, with unabashed
devotion and complete lack of concern about what people do for a
living, how much money they have, or how much they weigh. The
fact that we still live with dogs, even when we don't have to herd
or hunt our dinner, gives me hope for humans and canines alike."
- Oprah Winfrey

Soon we were on the move again, my dad, me, and a stray farm dog
that he brought with us. I'm not sure why he brought the dog. Maybe
he thought the dog would keep me company so he wouldn't have to be
bothered doing so. My dad later beat that dog so badly that it had to be
rescued. But that's later…

We moved to Texas to rejoin my Aunt Kathy and Uncle Steve, who
had just moved back. It was almost my tenth birthday, and that was a big
deal for me because it was a double digit. Getting to see them was a great
birthday present, and we had a happy reunion, just like a real family.

I remember driving with my uncle down Interstate Highway 75 in
Dallas. We passed by a Mrs. Baird's bread factory and I smelled the
delicious smell of "homemade" bread. The smell of fresh bread was so
comforting to me, maybe because getting that one piece of fresh, hot
bread was the only comfort I felt while making the drug runs in Mexico
with my mom. My favorite song, "Hotel California" by the Eagles, was
on the radio. I was so happy when I got the album for my birthday that I
memorized every word of every song.

We found an apartment in Texas and my dad enrolled me in school. I
was a latch key kid, returning from school to an empty home while my
father went to work doing construction. Of course, that was nothing new

for me because I was used to emotionally returning to an empty home whether he was there or not.

It was during that time that I discovered skateboarding, and I loved it. Other than short periods of time around my Aunt Kathy, I had no women to look up to as role models. My mother was a drug addict who tortured me, and my grandmother had become a drunk, so I had become a tomboy due to growing up around roughnecks, miners, and construction workers.

Our new apartment complex was shaped like a large square with a pool in the middle, and surrounded by a fence. There was a sidewalk on the outside of the fence that had poles at each corner. I would race to the end of the sidewalk, picking up speed, then grab the pole and spin the skateboard around the pole with all my momentum. It was such an exciting adventure riding a skateboard, and the fear of falling made it all the more thrilling. On one particular day, I wanted to see how fast I could go if I really tried. So I got going as fast as I could, when suddenly the skateboard went flying out from under me and crashed through someone's window. I grabbed the skateboard out of the broken window frame and ran to hide in my apartment. Thank God I was not hurt, and they were not home.

I could not tell my father I had broken the window. I feared that man with every fiber of my being. I had to be perfect around him, and even when I was perfect he still hurt me, let alone when I did something wrong. Can you imagine trying to be a perfect child and still getting beaten? I concluded that nothing I did was ever good enough, and even worse, that I was never good enough. That pattern of trying to be perfect to be loved plagued me into my adult years.

Each day, I would ride by this one guy's apartment because he would always say hi, and I liked the music he listened to. I craved love and attention, and he would just sit and watch me. It made me feel important, like someone cared. After some time, he invited me into his house. I'm not sure if I knew what was coming next, but I can understand why I would be drawn to it. The tragic truth was that *that was what I knew*. After my unwilling initiation into sex at age five at the compound in Oregon, followed by my father's incestuous acts, some part of my brain equated that with love and I was starved for it otherwise.

The man offered me some water and chips. After I accepted them, he let me know the price. He raped me. I just turned my head into the pillow and cried silently. I tried to leave when he was done, but he had his way with me several more times before he let me go. I felt so cheap, so dirty, and so ashamed. I cried until his pounding upon me stopped, and then I ran home to hide under my blanket. I was filled with fear and guilt.

I couldn't tell anyone what had happened. Worse yet, I had no one to tell. My father had done the same thing to me, and I had no other family except Uncle Steve. For some reason I was afraid that he wouldn't believe me. I also didn't want him to think less of me, or stop loving me. I was so consumed with shame that I believed it was somehow my fault. That guilt and the guy's threats to kill me if I ever told anyone kept his crime a secret until now. That is how a perpetrator controls their victim's mental state.

I pushed it down and tried to make it go away. I tried to go to school and have fun like a normal child. The only fun part I enjoyed was being away from home. Because I was forced to be an adult at a very young age, I struggled to connect with other children. My dirty little secrets kept me from ever getting close or feeling like I could "fit in." It was also a challenge for me because I was always around adults; I had no idea how to be a child. The "child" was stripped away from me years before.

CHAPTER 11

*"I can be changed by what happens to me.
But I refuse to be reduced by it."*
- Maya Angelou

I came home after school one day to the usual emptiness of my life. I pretended to walk in and hear, *"Hi, Honey! How was school?"* I invented imaginary words from a fantasy father. Instead, I heard someone in my dad's room making noises that excited and frightened me at the same time.

Who's here? Dad is at work.

I opened the door to find my father having sex with some woman. I was in shock, and just stood there until he snapped me out of it by grabbing me violently and sending me out the front door with the sound of his raging voice.

I ran and ran. I hid near a trashcan and waited for him to come and take me home. But, like before, my father never came to get me. Once again I had to come home with my head held down in shame. I could not look at him, and I could not find any words to say to him. I wasn't sure how I felt. Jealous, sick, abandoned...

The next day I came home from school to find something sitting on top of the TV. In a sick attempt to make things right, my father actually got me a gift. It was a vibrator. Yes, my father got me my own vibrator at the age of ten. The rules were, *"You can only use it in the living room, and you can only do it when I am here. It will make you feel good..."*

He showed me where it put it and how to use it, and I obliged out of the fear of angering him by refusing. When he was home, I would pull a blanket up over my waist and use it while he watched me. Physically, it did feel good, and I wanted so badly to feel good. I remember in the movie Monster's Ball there was a scene where Halle Berry just wanted to feel good, no matter what that meant. That was how I felt. So I would turn my head into the pillow and attempt to feel good on the outside, while the last shreds of my dignity and childhood died on the inside.

In an effort to seek any form of attention in my rebellious youth or premature adulthood, I decided I would start smoking cigarettes. When my father found out, he thought the best way to make me stop would be to put a full pack of Camels in my mouth with a rubber band wrapped around them to hold them in place. They were the kind with no filters (his cigarettes, the hypocrite). My jaw was open so wide it hurt. He lit them and put a pail over my head and had me the deepest breath I could. I choked, gagged and I threw up for days. Considering he was a chain smoker of unfiltered Camel's, it seemed insane that he would have a reaction to me smoking. I think deep down inside, as sick as it was, I felt like he actually cared.

I felt the same way when he would come in my room at night and poor whisky down my throat. He said it would help me sleep. He was really trying to make me pass out so he could have his way with me. Passing out or leaving my body was a better alternative than seeing the reality that my father was using me as his sex toy.

As much as I might have wished otherwise in some moments, life went on. I kept skateboarding, or "escape-boarding" as it really was for me, going to school, and hating my life. Eventually I made a couple of friends in the apartment complex...birds of a feather. They were twin brothers who had been abused like me. We were the unwanted, seeking solace in each other's company and an answer in each other's eyes to the question of "Why." An answer none of us had.

We were playing outside when I first saw the scars on their chests. I asked what happened and they said that their mother would burn them with hot tea when they were bad. Their pain was palpable. I felt it not from their chests, but from their hearts. I looked in their eyes and knew that "bad' was something their mother made up and likely changed from day to day. They didn't deserve that anymore than I did, or any child ever could. I felt sick inside.

Soon I met another friend in the apartment complex, a girl named Heather, who was deaf. She was much older than I, but she understood me...she got me. We spent a lot of time together. It was so great to go to her house and hang out. I would stay there as long as they would have me.

My new friend and I hung out every day. Her older sister shared a room with her, and late one night her sister brought her boyfriend home. They started having sex in her bed because she knew her sister could not hear it, but she did not know I was there. I giggled to myself at first because it was so funny to me, but then I felt a little aroused and really awkward. I felt that I was invading her privacy. I had no idea what to do, so I just lay there silently until morning. When she awoke and saw me there, she realized I had heard everything.

She looked at me with a terrified expression saying, *"Please don't tell on me."*

I understood her desires and yearning for love. I was just a little jealous that she got to experience it by choice with someone that she wanted to be with. I never told a soul, and she never spoke a word to me.

CHAPTER 12

"For what you do to others, you do to yourself."
- Eckhart Tolle

My dad found a new girlfriend, but she was not the one that I had walked in on with him. When he brought her home for the first time, I was enthralled with her. There was no jealousy at all. She was beautiful, she was kind, and she felt safe.

The only thought I had was, *"What in the hell is someone so nice and gorgeous doing with my dad?"*

She had long brown hair and big, beautiful brown eyes. She was a model in my eyes. I was so confused, why would she be with someone like my father? I quit asking myself that question before long and became like a little puppy around her.

"How do you make your hair curly like that?"

"How do you do your makeup?"

"How are you such a woman when I am such a tomboy?"

"Who taught you how to be a girl?"

I was in awe of her beauty, her mannerisms, and her womanly figure. She was so curvy, so gorgeous. I realize now that my infatuation with her was due to the fact that I had no female role models in my life. No motherly figure had ever shown me any attention or love. It was the illusion of a loving family unit that I became enamored with. I wanted to ask her, *"Will you be my mom and not hurt me and not leave?"*

The relationship with my father and his beautiful girlfriend, B.J., was getting serious. We moved into her home soon after dad nearly beat our dog to death. Remember the farm dog? We moved him from the wide-open spaces of the ranch in Minnesota to a tiny little apartment in Dallas with no room for him to run. The poor dog was miserable. I could not stop him from tearing things up, and I could not stop my dad from kicking the dog. I had never stood up to my father before, but when he was savagely beating that dog I jumped in the middle to spare the dog from my father's wrath. Who knew that I would be doing it again in the future?

Dad and BJ spent all their time together, and I had not one bit of jealousy because I loved her so much. Thankfully, I was no longer my father's sex toy either. BJ had two children, and I thought I would finally have a normal family. I was so happy I was getting a brother and sister. My new sister, Michelle, was ten years old like me, and my new brother, Sean, was nine.

When we moved in, I thought things were going to be great. In my mind I had dreams of unity and love, a brother and sister, a real family with the type of relationships that my heart so deeply desired. The reality was I had to share a room with Michelle, and she was not happy with that situation at all. Kids can be cruel, especially when they feel threatened by the arrival of a newcomer. I remember hiding in the closet when she would bring her friends over. They would talk about me and say things like:

"She just plays with boys."
"She looks like a boy."
"She's ugly and stupid."

I was so hurt. My fairy tale had already begun to crumble, and I had no one to talk to about it. I worshiped my new mom and didn't want her to hate me, so I said nothing. It did not take long for my already crumbling fairy tale of unity and love to collapse into the wreckage of pain and hatred. The torture started with food. When we sat at the table for dinner, if my father saw anything that we were eating around or that we did not like to eat, he would force us to eat it in large quantities. His intention was that we would eat it until we would somehow magically love it. This was the same twisted technique he used with the cigarettes, but somehow he expected it to have the opposite effect.

My nemesis was peas, and when he learned that, I had to eat a whole serving bowl full of them. He sat and watched me eat every single pea. It was all I could do to keep from throwing up. The fear of what he would do to me if I did was a powerful motivator to keep them down. As soon as I was excused from the table I ran to the bathroom and shut the door, barely making it to the toilet before they spewed from my mouth like a scene from the Exorcist. In a panic, I flushed the toilet and cleaned up as quickly as I could, lest I was caught.

Worse than that was the memory of Michelle, when she mistakenly revealed her disgust for sausage that is encased in the skin of I don't even want to know what. I felt so sorry for her as she gagged on every bite, tears rolling down her face. We sat there for hours until she finished it. It was torturous for us all, except for the head of the family: my father, the torturer.

I was so embarrassed and ashamed to be his daughter. I was so sad and sorry that we had come into their lives and created such a hell for them. I felt the anger and hatred that they felt towards my father and me. I could feel them shooting daggers at me with their eyes each time I was in their presence. They were kids and did not realize I was a victim too.

After we were settled in, dad went from food torture to beating Sean like a punching bag. Dad would beat him so badly that Sean would run and hide in the doghouse outside. There were times when I thought he was dead. I could see the pain and terror in BJ and Michelle's eyes, as if they had just invited Satan to live with them. I only wish I had been able to warn them in advance that they had.

We all began acting out and hitting each other. Our pain, fear, and rage needed expression and had no other avenue. Sean stabbed me with a fork. I hit him with a large board and knocked him out. He threw a croquet ball at Michelle. We were a product of our environment, which only became more painful and terrorizing by the minute.

CHAPTER 13

"Courage: the most important of all the virtues because without
courage, you can't practice any other virtue consistently."
- Maya Angelou

The depths of my father's depravity found new levels with what he called "Red Night".

He told us, *"Red Night is when I leave the door open to our bedroom and you kids are allowed to come into our bed."*

We thought ... or should I say we "hoped" we were going to "snuggle" with the family, all of us lying down together to watch a movie and bond. I don't know what made us think that we would be given this sudden reprieve from the nightmare that was our normal.

I soon concluded that it was called "Red Night," because it was bloody and painful. My father had named it for his sexual intentions. On "Red Night" my father decreed that we children were not only to watch our parents engaged in lewd sexual acts, we were to be active participants. My evil bastard of a father had oral sex with Michelle at the tender age of ten, but considering he had done this to me at eight years old, I only wish I was surprised. He forced his tongue into her pre-pubescent vagina, while he made Sean shove his entire arm into his mother's vagina. That was more than I could handle. I blacked out after I saw that, so I am unsure what happened to me. Probably more of the same. To this day, I don't remember what he did to me on "Red Night," but I do remember that it continued every week until we moved from that house.

Going to school and being "normal kids" was like walking a tight rope over an ocean of sharks waiting for you to fall. We walked out of our door, out of the gates of Hell, and into the storybook reality of other children's lives. We were to maintain a facade of being normal children within this alternate reality or suffer even further consequences. There were times of forced interaction with the other children in school. We would go to the skating rink, mandatory field trips where we were told to "play nice" with the others. I would seek attention from boys by being sexually flirtatious. I craved attention and didn't know any other way to get it.

I didn't know any other language to say, *"Can anyone see me? Can anyone love me? Can anyone just hug me without hitting me, hurting me, or raping me?"*

I found a new friend named Molly, whom I thought was just incredible. She had a big family with lots of brothers, a father who was a policeman, and a real mom, too. Like my old friend Heather at the apartments, I would stay with her and her family as much as I could. That was a safe place for me to sleep, and when I think of that now it makes my heart ache that a child would be happy and so relieved just to find a safe place to sleep. Shouldn't that just be a given that a child should have food, be loved, and have a safe place to sleep?

I never wanted to leave Molly's home. I would stay until they made me go home. When I had overstayed my welcome, I was sent on my way, her parents having no idea what they were sending me back to. The walk home was always a lonely, painful experience of dread. I never had any idea what new horror was waiting for me when I got home.

CHAPTER 14

"There are energy vampires everywhere. They can be your family, your friends, even your boundaries are your garlic. Love yourself enough to love garlic."
- Aleta Mackey

On the walk back to Hell one day, I saw a bus that was picking up a bunch of kids. I had no idea where it was going, but I got on. Nobody asked me any questions. I ran to the back of the bus and dug in, hoping that we were going somewhere far, far away and that nobody would notice I didn't belong until after we got there. I discovered at the end of our all too short journey that it was the bus for the local Baptist church. Not quite the salvation from Hell that I had hoped for, but I didn't care what kind of church it was, I just wanted anything to get me out of my house. They were willing to pick me up every week, and that was good enough for me.

But I soon found the message in that church disturbing and could not continue my attendance. The preacher screamed about hellfire and brimstone, and that we were all sinners who God would punish if we didn't do His bidding. It did not resonate in my heart that there was a Heavenly Father that would send his children to a place called Hell, where we would be tortured for eternity for displeasing Him. I already had that kind of father here on Earth. I was already in Hell, and the God that was in my heart *had* to be different. God loves me no matter what; he wouldn't give me choices and free will and then punish me for using them. My God loves me, my God is LOVE. In my heart I knew it to be true then, and I still do to this day.

We moved into an apartment and "Red Night" stopped, but the beatings took over. We could not sleep at night because the door to my parents' bedroom was connected to our bedroom, and my stepmom was tied to the door and getting whipped. Whether for pleasure or punishment I didn't know, but the screams I heard couldn't be described as pleasure in any corner of my imagination. After the beatings, they would have sex so loud that I am surprised no one called the police. Oh how I wish someone had called the police.

Dad was obsessed with chasing my stepsister Michelle through the house and terrorizing her until she would crawl into the closet with a migraine. Beatings took place daily, and we had the choice of a paddle with holes in it, a Ping-Pong paddle, a whip, a belt, or his hand. How generous of him to give us so many options. After I experienced them all, I quickly realized that the Ping-Pong paddle made a great noise, but did not hurt. However, I could not share this merciful secret with Michelle or Sean, or else my dad would figure it out and make me choose something else. The guilt I felt for not sharing was as emotionally painful as the physical pain of those beatings. So I was really granted no reprieve at all.

It wasn't much longer before my stepmother, BJ, couldn't take it anymore and confessed her plight to her parents, risking her own safety to get her children out of that hell. And so, Michelle and Sean were rescued. Their grandparents swooped in to save them...but no one came to save me. No one called my family. Oh yeah...what family? Uncle Steve and Aunt Kathy were the only sane people left who might care about me, but for whatever reason BJ didn't call them, the police, or anyone else that could have saved me from that hell.

So, with no heroes to come and pull me from the darkness, I was left alone, again. My fellow inmates, my compatriots in pain, the only ones who could understand what I was going through, were gone. They were granted a pardon and I was left with him. Left with the beatings, left with the abuse, left with the silence, left in the pits of Hell. I continued to placate him and submit to his every word, his every sick and twisted whim, in order to avoid more pain.

CHAPTER 15

"I love to see a young girl go out and grab the world by the lapels.
Life's a bitch. You've got to go out and kick ass."
- Maya Angelou

Dad and BJ decided to open a sign company, and for some time they were successful. That was good for me. The more they worked, the less time he had to pummel me. They were making money, and that, coupled with the distraction of the new business, created the illusion that we were semi-normal. It allowed me to go to school and begin to blend in as a normal child, or at least it made it easier for me to wear that mask.

We moved to Plano, Texas, a Dallas suburb known for its money and perfectly manicured lawns. The appearance of our lives was deceiving, so deceiving in fact, that I began to believe that my father had somehow changed. With our newly found financial means, my dad moved my grandmother out of the nursing home and into our home. My father was suddenly the loving son who cared about somebody's well being other than his own.

My grandmother's alcoholism was atrocious. She was a wretched drunk. The stench from the alcohol and thick fog from her cigarettes was overwhelming, but somehow the loving little child in me still wanted to be connected to her grandmother. Trying not to choke on the smell, I sought to bond with her and luckily she was usually too drunk to resist. I would cuddle up with her, even though she was like a big stuffed animal that mumbled and smelled like a seedy downtown bar. Still, there was something comforting about her cold hands wrapped around me at night while we slept together. It was like that feeling of flipping your pillow over to the cold side in the night. It calmed me from the outside in.

I was with her on the day that I started my period. I was not yet eleven, and not having been forewarned (as a normal daughter would have been by her mother), it was very traumatic for me.

"Grandma something's wrong. I am bleeding down there! Someone stabbed me, I am dying Grandma!"

Grandma just slurred, *"You're a woman now. I have to call all my friends. Here's a pad, put it in your panties."*

That was it. That was my initiation to womanhood. No description of what was going on with my body, no consolation, nothing. So now I am a woman at eleven years of age. Bleeding, hurting, and wearing a diaper. I appealed to BJ for information about what was happening to me. She at least offered some explanation, but she left out one important factor: my sex drive was now in full force. As if it wasn't before.

"Houston, we have a problem."

The abuse in the family switched directions after my stepbrother and sister moved out. I was spared from his sexual and physical abuse. I don't know if it was mercy, boredom, or fear of being caught by my grandmother, but I was relieved. Dad began beating BJ, but Grandma was usually too drunk to notice or care.

One night I could hear BJ screaming and crying. I walked into the living room to find her holding a bag to her mouth, breathing in and out, hyperventilating. My dad was on the couch, out cold.

I timidly asked, *"What are you doing?"*

She said, *"Your dad did some cocaine and then took some sleeping pills and passed out. I am so angry, Aleta! I want to beat him, and that is what I am going to do!"*

And so she did. Standing over him, she balled up her fists and began driving them into his face. Blood sprayed from his mouth and nose. For a moment I watched with pleasure for all the times he had beaten us, but that was mixed with the pain of whatever patriarchal bond I still felt towards him. I did not want to see anymore dysfunction, so I simply went to my room and closed the door. Oddly enough, I remember that there were no consequences suffered the next day. He either didn't remember what had happened, or somehow understood that he deserved it. Probably the latter.

CHAPTER 16

"Being unwanted, unloved, uncared for, forgotten by
everybody, I think that is a much greater hunger, a much
greater poverty than the person who has nothing to eat."
- Mother Teresa

During the time that my dad had the sign business, I would go to the shop and help paint the signs. There was an employee there named Danny. I thought he was so hot, and I wanted him so badly. I was only eleven, but according to Grandma, I was a woman. I did everything I could to get him to want me.

He told me one day, *"Aleta, you're a little girl and I am a man. Men do not touch little girls like that."*

He had no idea what an impact that had on my life. He was the one and only man that did the right thing and let me be a little girl. I had no idea how to relate to men other than to try to seduce them. Using my body for attention was what I knew. The success of the sign company was so incongruent with the failure of our family life. It was only a matter of time before the outer mirrored the inner once more. Soon after we moved to Plano, they lost the business and we moved again to a dingy apartment on the bad side of Dallas. Grandma threw a fit at the news she'd have to move back to the assisted living home, but she threw drunken fits all the time. Dad showed little emotion at the separation.

We moved from beautiful Plano to the "bad" neighborhood where I was one of the only white girls in the school. Some dysfunctional boys saw this fragile little white girl as a nice target for sexual abuse. When I would walk to my classes, three of them would circle me in the hallway like sharks around a wounded seal. They would grab my breasts and my butt while insulting and bullying me.

"Where you going, bitch? You're a whore, aren't you? You want this

dick, don't you whore? You know you want this black dick! Are you ignoring me, bitch? Don't you fucking ignore me! I'll whoop your ass!"

Even though my father was a huge racist, I was not. I did not see that as a black/white issue, but rather a case of bullying and control. I felt completely separated and targeted. They would follow me with more of the same when I walked home from school. I was terrified and didn't know what to do, so I just tried to keep walking as if they weren't there. One day they pushed me down in somebody's front yard and shoved my face in the grass while they felt me up. I don't know if they would have raped me if we were not in such a public place, or if they only wanted to humiliate me and have power over me. But humiliated I was. After violating me with their hands and words they walked away, laughing to themselves, while I was left with a mouth full of dirt and grass and eyes full of tears and rage. I knew I would need to find protection soon if I was going to survive in that neighborhood.

As I said, my father was a racist, among his other endearing qualities, so I knew I could not go to him and tell him what was going on. If I had, there would have been some dead boys. No matter what they had done to me, I couldn't wish death on any human being. I made several attempts to get the principal to help me stop the unmerciful bullying, but he offered me no help. I felt invisible and ashamed for something I did not do. That was my first attempt to ask for help from the outside world, and I was made to feel like a slut. I gave up.

I realized that the only one who could stop it was me. I started by keeping a roll of quarters in my pocket to hit them with, but I was outnumbered and unskilled, so that was unsuccessful. I took a knife to school figuring, *"Kill or be killed,"* but that was also unsuccessful because I just couldn't hurt someone that way. I tried to fight back by kicking and hitting, but again, I had no fighting skills and could not fight the numerous boys that wanted their way with me.

So I decided to learn how to fight. I signed up for the boxing team at school. They did not have any girls on the team, but I convinced the coach that I could do it. I had so much built-up rage that once I started letting that energy out, it was like tearing the lid off of Pandora's Box. It came out strong, so strong that I wanted more. I became the first girl boxer in our school, and I was undefeated, fighting only boys.

Unfortunately, they stopped the boxing program after a couple of months. That was really disappointing to me. Boxing allowed me to release the pain within my soul and it helped me protect myself from my aggressors. I knew it was only a matter of time before the hyenas would begin circling again, so I turned to the only other way that I knew to protect me, my sexuality.

I found an older boyfriend in high school to protect me (I was still in grade school). He would meet me in the morning to walk me to school and then he would pick me up after school. Between my limited boxing skills and his age and size, the boys who had made me their "little white whore" retreated back into the shadows or found another victim.

CHAPTER 17

"Although the world is full of suffering,
it is full also of the overcoming of it."
- Helen Keller

One day as I was walking to meet my new high school boyfriend, I looked through a fence and on the other side was a man with a painters mask on. He was not painting however; he was masturbating and ejaculating all over the fence. I ran back home and told my stepmom. She called the police and they said that they had been looking for this man because he had raped a little boy in the neighborhood.

I was terrified, as I still had to walk alone through this area to meet my boyfriend. As I was walking, I looked over at the tree beside me and saw a painters mask hanging from a limb. I took off and ran faster than I think I ever had. I was afraid that with my past experience with rape and sexual abuse, I would attract this man like a magnet. I thank God that I never encountered him again and the police finally did arrest him. I hope he got the maximum sentence for the torture that little boy experienced.

Sometime after that we needed money, and my dad realized his mother had a hefty inheritance from my grandpa, which he and my Uncle Steve were next in line to inherit. So he set his sights on her as his next cash cow. The problem was that Uncle Steve had power of attorney over the estate. He had taken over the finances years ago after grandma had to be put in a home for her alcoholism. Dad was too much of a vagabond to be put in charge or take any responsibility, so Uncle Steve had. Now my father's own flesh and blood was an obstacle to getting his hands on the cash. His evil gears started turning as he talked about ways to get to the money. He realized he either had to kill his own mother, which would prove too difficult with her living in the nursing home, or he had to get to his brother.

He set his plan in motion by inviting Steve over for dinner one night. Steve was a good man, always happy to connect with his family, so he, of course, accepted. Once he was there, dad slipped something into Steve's drink and drugged him. When I saw Steve acting strangely at the table, I knew something wasn't right.

My dad and BJ looked at each other with an expression that told me that they had planned the whole thing. I was afraid for Uncle Steve and wanted to protect him, but my dad had other plans.

He looked at me and said, *"It's time for you to go to bed."*

His face and tone let me know that it was not open for discussion, so I excused myself and went to my room. My heart sank as I realized my heartless bastard of a father was easily capable of killing his own brother.

In the morning, I was relieved to discover that Steve was not dead. I don't know what happened that night, but I do know that Steve signed the power of attorney over to my dad soon after that. I didn't see Steve around very much after that night, and I hated my dad just a little bit more for how he had manipulated that good man.

So now we had money, and taking care of priorities first, BJ got a boob job. I was so angry! There I was wearing high-water pants and had holes in my shoes and clothes that we bought at Goodwill three years ago, but she got new boobs. But to my dad, he was just investing in his new business: BJ the Stripper.

With BJ working as a topless dancer, my father had full access to unlimited alcohol throughout the day, all the topless women he desired, and free babysitting by throwing me in the dressing room with the rest of the "bitches." As the husband of the top dancer at the club, he was the head cock of the roost; a brilliant plan for a man of his tendencies. I would hang out in the dressing room and watch the dancers do cocaine, complain about their miserable lives, and talk about how they hated the men that came in the club. I watched as their lives spiraled downward into a circle of self-induced misery. Of course, all of that only served to feed the alcohol-fueled darkness in my father, which was probably the root of his plan all along.

One night BJ came upstairs to my room.

"Aleta, wake up! Your dad is passed out! We need to leave now! We have to jump from the window and run!"

We were on the second floor, and my window opened onto a section of the roof that slanted down to the gutter over the front door. It was no more than a seven-foot drop, and one that she obviously thought we could handle. We were both petrified with fear at the possibility of being caught. I was unable to move. She volunteered to go first and started sliding down the roof. Trying her best to slide silently, her feet dangled over the edge of the rain gutter as she searched for a handhold. Suddenly, my dad's hands reached up like a scene from a scary movie, grabbed her feet, and dragged her over the edge as she screamed and clawed at the tile as she slid to her doom. He had obviously been aware of her plan and was waiting at the front door.

He dragged her into the house by her hair and the beating began. I lay in bed, crying, feeling every painful blow she received. As I listened to her cries and the hard, smacking thud of fist on flesh, I knew that it would be the first and last escape attempt she would make for us.

As you can probably guess, my father quickly burned any bridges he had built and wore out his welcome at the strip club. BJ lost the exalted position of "top dancer" when she kept coming to work with black eyes and bruises, so his latest business venture soon failed like all the rest. My father's friend from the Navy, Dwaine, suggested we come up to Minnesota after we lost the sign business because he had an idea of what we could do for work. That, combined with the idea of getting out of town before the law or a lynch mob came after my dad, put us back on the road again.

CHAPTER 18

"If we have no peace, it is because we have
forgotten that we belong to each other."
- Mother Teresa

Dad moved BJ and me to Ely, Minnesota. Their small town claim to fame is that Bob Dylan began his singing career there, or at least that's what they say. Minnesota in the wintertime is cold...really cold. We're talking icicles hanging off your nostril hairs, cold. We moved to an island on Shagawa Lake, and the only access was a small bridge about three feet wide with no railing or handholds. When it froze over you had to slide on your butt to get to the mainland. The island had a cabin. A cabin with no running water, no electricity, but it did have an outhouse. We had no bathroom, no bathtub, and I was thirteen years old. Let's just say I was less than thrilled.

Somehow, we survived the winter. In fact, we became clever and downright ingenious. We emptied the closet and stapled plastic garbage bags to the inside of it. Then we put a drain in the bottom of the floor, got a 20-gallon jug and attached a shower hose onto the end, and used it as our shower. Oh wait, it gets better. Where we showered, we also shit. We bolted a toilet seat to the inside of the closet, got a large pale, lined it with a garbage bag, and put it under the toilet seat. That, versus the icy cold of the outhouse, was heaven my friends.

It turns out that Dwaine's business idea was that we could rent out canoes from the island in the spring and summertime, and in return, live there in the cabin year round. Hardly a profitable venture, but it allowed us to live. BJ got a job as a bartender in the local bar, which allowed my dad to continue his drinking, and I was enrolled in the local school.

I was guarded, shy, and scared from my past experiences. I had no idea what to expect. I was told that I must wear a dress and heels the first day of school. I was a tomboy, and that news terrified me because of my past sexual harassment at the school in Dallas. I felt like I was walking into a dog pound wearing Milk-Bone underwear.

That first day, I clomped down the hall with that awkward walk, which made it painfully apparent to everyone that I had never worn heels before. I walked into class a bit late because I could not find my classroom, and because any movement was slow going in that get up. When you're late, all eyes are on you as you enter. Doing my best to gather my composure, I began to hobble to my desk as best I could in those evil shoes, when my ankle suddenly twisted in refusal to be a part of the charade any longer. I fell down in front of everyone, and my skirt flipped over my head, which gave everyone in class a look at my lovely panties. Thank God they bought me panties. It was so embarrassing; I was mortified.

But after that, school actually became fun for me. The other kids thought I was the most fascinating thing they had ever met. I was from Dallas when the television show of the same name was so popular. I was the daughter of this 'big tittied' bartender, the only female bartender in that little podunk town. So not only was I the hot new topic, I was actually popular!

I even got a boyfriend! His name was Dick (yeah, I know). He was attracted to me because I was distant, mysterious, and gave great head (hey, with a boy named Dick it was an easy segue). Obviously, I still used sex as my power to keep men in my life. I thought it was the only valuable quality I had. Sex had been part of my life for as long as I could remember.

Dick wasn't someone that I would normally be attracted to. He was a jock, and was genuine and sincere. I usually picked the bad boys that treated me poorly, mirroring my daddy issues. But Dick actually treated me with kindness and love, and it was beautiful. I remember just having fun with him riding snowmobiles through the forest, holding onto him for dear life with the icy wind hitting my face, and loving every minute of it. We would meet after school at the library and he filled my heart. Life was good! A boyfriend, tag football, kids being around…I felt normal. Not that I knew what normal was, but I thought I felt it, and it felt good.

CHAPTER 19

"As selfishness and complaint pervert the mind,
so love with its joy clears and sharpens the vision."
- Helen Keller

As much as I was healing there on the island, I was still self-medicating all of the past pain that kept rising up, that ruined the peace I felt there. Remember, I had been getting high since I was force-fed marijuana tea and butter and hash brownies as a toddler to keep me quiet. What kid doesn't love brownies? I was just a kid who was given brownies filled with hash. With the fine role models of my father and grandmother, alcohol was as available and acceptable for me to drink as Kool-Aid, probably more so. The same was true of the drugs. I started smoking pot when I was about eleven. Dad had it in his room, easy to find and easy to use.

When at home in the cabin, I would listen to The Animals album by Pink Floyd while smoking peyote and going to other dimensions. I really felt I was tapping into the Native American Indian energy and using it with purpose. At thirteen, I was going on self-initiated vision quests using peyote and going out into nature to connect with Spirit. I found peace living on that island. Taking the time to be with nature renewed my spirit. I found my sanctuary in fishing, canoeing, and exploring the island. It was a forest, and on the back of the island there was a huge, tree-surrounded boulder that overlooked the lake. Simply gazing at the lake that went on for miles was the true song, the essence of my soul...still water, still heart, peace and quiet.

I would take my homework to the back of the island, sit on that boulder to study, then pause, breathe, and take it all in. The smell of the fresh air; all of the sensations that come from connecting with nature; tapping into God. I was thriving for the first time in many years. I was getting filled up; my heart was no longer empty. Even my parents seemed to be perfectly placed out of my life, for every time I would return home, they were never there. It was if I had a refuge on that island. I was healing, inside and out.

While on the big rock on the back of the island, I was able to observe a bear family and a deer family. I would just sit and watch, and they never attempted to hurt me. I felt a real kinship with them, like we were one. When the ice cleared, I would pack my lunch and take my leaches (leaches are used as bait to catch walleye) out to fish for the day. I loved being on that island in the spring. I loved the nature, I loved the water, and *I loved me*. I was getting straight A's in school, I had a real boyfriend, and I felt alive.

There were so many times in the past when I would finally begin to settle into something stable, even if it was just being in an apartment for longer than 6 months, when my father would turn it upside down with his evil and alcoholism and begin the beatings on me and my stepmom once again. I was finally finding peace in my life after so many years of turmoil. I felt alive. I felt loved. But happiness and relief were always temporary with my father, and it was all soon to be taken away.

One night my father came home with BJ after she had finished her shift at the bar in town. They were drunk, as usual. My father was belligerent, as usual, and BJ was embarrassed yet again. They were fighting, and dad began hitting her. When I saw her pain under the force of his fists, it was impossible for me to just sit and do nothing. I knew that I would receive the beating in her place, but it no longer affected me as it once did. Sadly, I wasn't as afraid of it because I was so used to it. So I put on my Wonder Woman cape and darted to her rescue. But this time, instead of being met by a fist, I was met by a shotgun to my head. I remember hearing the distinctive CHIK-CHIK sound of him chambering a round against my forehead before I blacked out. Locked and loaded...

The next day I woke to BJ packing our stuff. We were on our way back to Texas. I wasn't dead, I wasn't shot, and I wasn't Aleta. I was numb. There's only so much pain and trauma that one can take before something inside just flips the switch to the "off" position. I didn't get to say goodbye to my boyfriend, my bear and deer families, or any other healed piece of me that I left behind on that beautiful island.

CHAPTER 20

"At fifteen life had taught me undeniably that surrender, in its place,
was as honorable as resistance, especially if one had no choice."
- Maya Angelou

I began to use drugs more frequently once we were back in Texas. I was thirteen years old and I loved that my friends thought it was cool that we could get high at my house. Like any teen seeking acceptance and attention, I wanted to be cool. I wanted to be loved.

Drugs were a way for me to numb my existence in the world of pain in which I was a prisoner, created by my parents and the other sick, dysfunctional adults that abused or violated me.

It was such a bitter, cold, non-loving environment, that I needed to numb myself to make it through each day. I can't say that I did not like drugs, because I did. I think most people do on some level or they wouldn't do them, but I can't say that I liked what they did to my spirit, to my mind, or to my consciousness. The drugs I was partaking in slowly caused a transformation over my body temple and spirit, not in a bright and sunny, "happy-joy-joy" way, but in a way that I did not even realize was happening. I have to say that marijuana was not a gateway drug for me as so many say it is, but alcohol was. I would never consider doing any kind of drug unless I had been drinking. Pot and alcohol did not mix for me.

My father stopped sexually abusing me after a while; I guess I'd just lost that new car smell. But the trauma was not over for me yet.

One night my dad, BJ, and I were in the living room with a friend of dad's, drinking and getting high while playing the game of Risk. Not your average family game night. I don't think most parents do shots and pass joints with their thirteen-year-old daughters. In the middle of the game, dad and BJ got up and said they were going to bed. I started to get up and my dad's friend (I don't even remember his name) grabbed my hand and kept me from leaving.

Dad looked back with an evil grin and said, *"No. You keep playing. The game is just getting good."*

He winked at his friend, went to his room, and closed the door behind him. Suddenly I realized that the game was over and I was the prize. To the victor go the spoils. To the victim goes another scar on her tattered psyche.

That became a regular thing...my dad letting his "good" friends come over and have me. He would just leave me in the living room with men and go to bed as if it was no big deal. He just left his child in the den with the big bad wolf. No wait, I forgot, that's you, Dad.

CHAPTER 21

"Courage is the most important of all the virtues,
because without courage you can't practice any
other virtue consistently. You can practice any virtue
erratically, but nothing consistently without courage."
- Maya Angelou

When I was thirteen, I had a girlfriend named Norma of the same age, and I think almost as damaged as me. She introduced me to a man named Frenchman who was my father's age, but who was, thank God, outside of my father's circle of friends. Frenchman never wanted to have sex with me, he just loved me; at least the closest thing to love that I had experienced. He gave me drugs. He just wanted me to be with him, he wanted me to fill the void of his lonely heart.

Frenchman enjoyed watching me when I would take mescaline. Mescaline is a form of peyote that makes you hallucinate like LSD. He would give me my own full eyedropper and I would put the drops under my tongue. I really loved the world that I went into when I was tripping. Laughter, complete joy, oneness with nature—that was where I wanted to resonate all the time.

But my girlfriend Norma and I would also do drugs together when we weren't with Frenchmen (our guardian angel), and men would sexually take advantage of our intoxicated states.

One night when Norma and I were using mescaline, we walked down a road when a rainstorm began. I started laughing so hard because the rain appeared to be going through my hand. The laughter continued for hours, and when we returned to her home, we went and hid in Norma's room because we were afraid her mother would find us tripped out and high. Her little Chihuahua came in to see what we were doing and started barking nonstop. As we looked at it, the little yapper appeared to suddenly grow a giant bobble head. We were laughing so hard we woke Norma's mother. She came in, but we still couldn't stop laughing.

She accused me of taking her daughter down a twisted path of drugs and sex; she was convinced it was all my fault. Little did her mother know that her daughter was the instigator on most of our excursions. I thought it was very hypocritical of her mother, especially considering we had just found a bag of cocaine in her mom's closet a few days before. As a mother, I now understand that you don't want your child to follow in your footsteps.

One night I decided to take Frenchman to meet my parents. I don't know what I was thinking.

Maybe I thought my dad would say, *"Aleta, what are you doing with a man my age? Stay home, go to school, create a life, become something, have a desire, a dream. I love you."*

Wow, I must have really been tripping to think he would ever say anything like that. My dad not only didn't say anything like that, he suggested I spend as much time as I wanted with him, because he would be at the topless bar.

We were living at the Circle Motel on Harry Hines in Dallas. If anyone knows Dallas, they know that motel. It is a drugged out, prostitute-filled, hellhole of a motel that no child should ever be near. I was told I didn't have to go to school; basically I could stay in that "lap of luxury," left to find something to do with my time and my life in such an undesirable environment.

Oh, daddy didn't have to worry, because I found so many things to do. I found a guy (not Frenchman) that forced me to suck his dick and then stuck a needle in my arm. As my eyes rolled back in my head, I embarked upon what seemed to be my most profound drug experience to date. The drug was methamphetamine, and after the initial rush I came back into my body and felt like I had jet fuel running through my veins. So I ran. I ran and ran and ran until I ended up in front of a convenience store. I saw this woman who had needle track marks up and down her arms, and she came up to me immediately. Again, like attracts like.

"You are a fat little girl. Come with me to see this doctor. He will give us the pills we need to get high."

Not only was I not fat, I saw her for who she really was…ME—if I did not turn myself around somehow. She was an angel in an addict's body, and she gave me a sign to run.

64

CHAPTER 22

"So go ahead. Fall down. The world looks different from the ground."
- Oprah Winfrey

Our next move was from Dallas to Key West, Florida. We traveled in a Good Times Van with a tiny little trailer attached. I guess we were running to some new job, or running from the same old circumstances. The drive was so long. We drove for hours and hours, and we were still in Texas, and I was angry. I was still filled with rage at the thought that I did not get to say goodbye to my boyfriend and have closure with the island in Minnesota. I refused to speak, and I refused to eat. When we made a food stop, I decided it would be a great time to try and kill myself. I swallowed as many black mollies (speed) as I could and used beer to wash them down. By the time they came back from their greasy burgers and fries, I was almost dead. I had chosen suicide inside the Good Times Van in the 103-degree summer heat in Texas with all the doors and windows closed. I was cooking and I was dying.

All I remember is being dragged to the bathroom and my stepmom being so pissed that she shoved a toothbrush down my throat until I puked. I wasn't sure if she was pissed because I almost died, or because I had taken all of her drugs. I like to think that she was scared for me and anger was the easiest emotion to expel. I know she loved me the best she could. We were both held hostage in dungeon of my father's psychosis.

We finally made it to Key West and parked our trailer in a trailer park that was right next to the ocean. The beauty of the sea gave me sanctuary, as well as a tiny bit of thanks that my suicide attempt was unsuccessful. There was something so calming about that place and the grace of each wave; it just seemed to know its place in the world. It had power, and yet it was balanced with calm and tranquility.

We moved into a dilapidated old mobile home that may have been older than the sea itself. I had my own room with a closet that had a manhole-sized section rotted out of the floor. I saw it as my own private entrance and exit for myself, and any raccoons that may have wanted to join me for a bedtime snack.

I began babysitting the neighbor's kids. I loved children. I knew I was going to be a mother someday. I knew if I were a mother, I would love that baby with the angel's kisses it deserved—that I had always desired. One afternoon I went to babysit at a neighbor's place, but when I knocked on the door the children's mother did not answer. The uncle did. He told me to come in and that he would be leaving shortly. He left directly after pinning me against the wall and raping me. I must have had a neon sign on my forehead that said "VICTIM" or "EASY TARGET" radiating a beacon to every sick pervert within a thirty-mile radius of me. Unable to stop him, I turned my head in shame until he had finished and left. Then I went on babysitting the children that night as if nothing had happened.

In my mind, nothing had really happened that wasn't a normal occurrence in my life. I was so numb at that point that nothing seemed to evoke any emotion in me at all, other than the excitement I felt when I thought of running away from all of it. The problem was that *I* seemed to be anywhere that *I* went, so therefore *I* needed to keep running from myself, which was obviously futile.

One day I decided to make a run for it, after my father said I could not spend the weekend with a friend of mine. After all the years of him not giving a shit about me, of him never caring what I did, him suddenly saying "No" just seemed like a power play. I was not ok with that at all.

When had he ever acted like a parent to me? It sure as hell wasn't going to start then. He hadn't earned the right to act like my father! Just because he spread his seed doesn't mean that he was really a father, especially when he spread that seed in his own child! A father is loving, accepting, nurturing, guiding, and shows their child examples of all of these things on a daily basis, as well as loving yourself. Those were not qualities that my father even knew existed.

So I packed my bag and snuck out of the hole in the floor of my room. I went to my friend's house and spent the night there, enjoying every rebel moment of it. Dad did not know where she lived or her phone number, so they knew nothing of my whereabouts. Nor do I feel that in between sipping his whiskey and smacking around my stepmom that he had the slightest concern or even a fleeting thought about my disappearance. My stepmom was probably worried, but would not take action because she was a beaten down, weak woman. She had attempted once to get me out of that hellhole, so maybe she thought I'd be better off on my own than living with them. I was free and I loved it.

My two friends and I decided to take a late night walk after a storm, just to feel the change in energy that occurs in the air after a good rain. We were dodging puddles and smelling the crisp air. As we went to walk around one puddle, one friend decided to walk through it. I thought we were all aware of the electrical pole that had fallen in the water. Suddenly I heard a loud pop, and I looked back to see a bolt of lightning run up from the ground through my friend. I fell to the ground in disbelief as she kept walking forward out of the puddle even though she had just been electrocuted. We walked her home and tried to talk to her, but she wasn't connecting with us, she couldn't speak. We told her parents what had happened and they rushed her to the hospital. She was brain damaged from the shock, and from that time on she was never the same.

I went back to my friend's house that I had run away to, but after what had happened, her parents told me to go home. But I didn't go home. I couldn't go home, so I went to another friend's house in downtown Key West. I stayed with her as long as I could, as long as her parents would let me. I think we made up some story that my parents were out of town as to why I needed to stay. I continued going to school, trying to keep up pretenses and do everything right. I created a pattern of attempting to be perfect that I still have ingrained in me. In my mind, if perfection still gets you beat down, then anything less than perfect must be death.

When the police came to school to get me, I knew my stepmom had called to find out if I had been attending and to report I was missing. Wow, a sign of love. It felt good, but a little too late. My heart was armored and numb, and nothing was penetrating that barrier, at least not then.

I had to quit going to school in order to avoid being sent back to my father's alcoholism and abuse. My friend's family began to ask questions about why I wasn't going home, so I left. Rather than go back to the den of the devil himself, I chose to be homeless at the age of thirteen. I would find places to sleep and eat for a small price: my mouth or my hand if they offered drugs with the meal and shelter. I really did not care any longer what was happening to me as long as I didn't have to return to my father.

But that life was a painful existence, too. Being homeless as a child is a very scary and painful place to be. I understood why there were so many children that ended up in prostitution. Their home life was probably a hell like mine, so far away from the functional fantasy world of *Leave It To Beaver*, and straight into the dredges of the *Jerry Springer* rejects. I wondered if any of the other runaways had a father like mine. Many of us ran together on the streets, a rag tag band of orphans. We never really talked about our families. We wanted to walk with blinders on and never look back. We just numbed ourselves and blended in with the others.

The police eventually found me and returned me home to the loving reception of a whiskey bottle and fists to my head.

CHAPTER 23

*"I'm not the average girl from your video, and I
ain't built like a supermodel, but I learned to love
myself unconditionally, because I am a queen."*
- India Arie

Soon, and seemingly without reason, we went back to Texas. I never
really understood what the attraction to Texas was. There seemed to
be some sort of magnet that always took us back there. It certainly
wasn't the most beautiful place in the world. I can think of so many
other states I wanted to explore, but Texas was always home.

I was fourteen years old and still not going to school. I was bored out
of my mind with my daily existence. Boredom is not a good thing for
anyone, let alone a teenage girl filled with hormones, and my whores
were moaning all right. I wanted to fill that void within my heart, that
empty feeling of just wanting someone to hold me, hit me, choke me,
anything...just validate my existence.

I had grown my hair to the longest it had ever been. When I was a
child, my grandmother was always fond of the shag haircut for me,
which was jagged and short and made me look like a boy. When we
went to the hair salon or barber she always shouted, *"Give 'er the shag!"*
Well, grandma wasn't around, and I was a young woman (or so I
thought) who was tired of looking like a boy. I had beautiful, long,
strawberry blonde hair, all one length. I was so proud of my new
feminine style.

I decided to make my way around the apartment complex to meet the
neighbors, at least the ones that offered drugs to fourteen-year-old girls.
There were more of those men than you might think. I also made a new
girl friend in my apartment complex. She was about twenty

years older than me, but she was very sweet. She and I would smoke pot together and she was the first person that I ever told about my life with my father. She could not believe that that kind of abuse actually existed in this world. She would let me stay at her house as much as she could, but she did not call the cops. Looking back at it now, I can only guess she was afraid to say anything.

My stepmom once told me that on one occasion she walked to the store to get some cigarettes, and when she returned the house was in complete darkness. She looked at my father sitting in a chair with the lights off and she described his eyes as "the portal to hell,"

"What are you doing sitting in the dark?" she asked.

He looked up at her and she was frozen by his stare. *"I sold my soul to the Devil to get my daughter back."*

She realized then that there was no hope for him, or us. She and I would be dead if we remained within the grasp of that devil.

I knew I had to get out of there. One day, these two guys asked me to take a walk with them. Always hoping someone would protect me, I decided to go along. I didn't have any shoes on, and when they took me to a field instead, I was terrified. That walk was not taking me to a place to be protected, nor was I going to be showered with love and affection or gold and gems by those two men. I knew that was going to be the place they raped and killed me.

I suddenly stepped on a bamboo shoot that got stuck in my toe.

Crying, I looked into one man's eyes with a tearful begging plea: *"Please take me home."*

And they did. Somehow, the man saw or felt my plea and changed his mind. He returned to his light and set me free.

Once home, I heard the screams yet again and rushed into another night of putting on my Wonder Woman cape to stop my dad from beating my stepmom. I figured I could at least take the blows for her so she could crawl away from him. But that night seemed different; my father seemed to be going deeper and deeper into the darkness. First, he pulled the pistol and put it to my head, then realized what would hurt me more was my hair. He knew how much I loved my hair, so he grabbed a large handful at the root on the back of my head and ripped it out.

He laid it on the cabinet and said, *"You are a slut, nothing but a slut. You are nothing to me, and don't you forget it. Anytime you forget who you are, look at this hair and remember."*

I could not believe that I had a bloody bald spot on the back of my head the size of a baseball, and my hair was just staring at me, crying. I was crying too, but on the inside. He was not going to see me cry. I was boiling inside. I felt this burning anger inside of me that was stronger than anything I had ever felt before.

There was a fire in my stomach that could not be suppressed any longer. All the beatings, all the rapes, the indifference that had gone on for so long, but that night was different. I knew that was the end of my life with him, or very soon it would be the end of me. With each beating, each gun to my head, each violation of my body, and each injustice to my soul, I was closer and closer to leaving this earthly plane, unable to take any more abuse.

I ran to my friend's house and showed her what he had done.

"Drive, just drive. Please, drive."

We drove and I cried, then I looked out the window and there *he* was...like a prince on his horse. I saw these two guys driving on the road beside us, waving us down to pull over. The driver was a friend of hers, so we pulled over. The passenger was a guy named Wes, who was cute enough, and even if he wasn't he would do. I was embarrassed by my bald spot and my current state of being an emotional wreck. I looked at Wes in the passenger seat and I said to myself:

"This is it. This is my out."

I put on my sex appeal, told him I was eighteen, and he picked me up later that night at my friends' house on his Harley. Riding away on that Harley with the wind in my hair, chilling my bald spot, I thought about my life with my father. There was not one moment of that ride that I didn't know to the depths of my soul that any hell was better than the hell of my father. To be free from my father would be worth living on the streets if I had to.

After I escaped, I learned that BJ found her way out by taking off with a drug dealer while my dad sat in a jail cell after getting arrested for fighting at the topless bar she worked at. We both were finally free of Walter Mackey.

CHAPTER 24

"Cause he is the truth, Said he is so real,
and I love the way that he makes me feel."
- India Arie

Wes was my ticket out, so I used whatever sexual magic I had to capture his heart and penis. I needed him to invest his time, energy, and sperm in me. Getting pregnant would seal the deal, but in the meantime I had to numb the nightmares that played in my head every day.

At first I was just smoking pot. I had no idea my new man was a former meth addict and was into the needle. When I met him he had quit doing meth, but that changed in time. That relationship had started out as me using him for my escape from hell, but I fell in love with him. Wes made me laugh, and he loved me the best that he could.

I thought I would never go back there...back to the needle, but I soon found myself with him in his ex-girlfriend's house with a needle in my arm and that chemical warmth running through my body once again. That was the ultimate high, and it was scary how good it felt. I was back in that space of knowing that the high was so incredibly life altering that I had no choice but to stop or keep going until I died.

To give you an idea of how quickly my life spiraled out of control on drugs (especially meth), a month later my father was out of jail, fucking Wes's ex-girlfriend in the bathroom, while I sat on the bed wondering how in hell he was back in my life.

A week later, we were driving drunk around the curvy, Austin hill country with my father at the wheel. In the backseat was a stranger we picked up along the way to Hippie Hollow (a nudist beach in Austin). As I watched the trees go by and held myself closely to Wes, I looked at my father, then back at Wes, and I realized I had picked my father all over again. That realization was a swift kick in the ass. I had gravitated to the familiar, and had no idea how disastrous that choice would turn out to be.

That day all I wanted to do was smoke some pot, lay in the sunshine, and pretend I wasn't present in that reality, but we didn't have any pot. I started visualizing in my mind what I wanted and how it would feel to get high. Then I looked down on the walking trail, and there was an envelope labeled 'skunk.' I opened it up and there was my manifestation. It was the first time I connected the power of my thoughts to the created world around me.

Later that week, after getting high, we decided that it would be an excellent time to go tubing down the river, right after a flooding rainstorm. Sheer genius. How much common sense does it require to realize that when the river is flooded with the floodgates open, it takes an act of God to stop your tube safely? Obviously a little more common sense than we had in our chemically enhanced think tank.

So there I was, stoned, scared shitless, and speeding down the white water rapids of a flooded river. In the distance I saw a bridge that was approaching much faster than I would have liked. I realized that it might be the only chance I had to stop before reaching the Gulf of Mexico. I decided to aim as best I could for one of the support columns. I knew the impact was going to suck, but it was the best chance I had to keep from drowning miles down the river.

The next thing I knew I was knocked unconscious and underwater with my body pinned against the column by the tube. I was drowning. The current was so strong that my bikini was ripped from my body. I was helpless to free myself from the stone column and certain death. I'm not sure how long I was there before I noticed I was observing myself from outside my body. My lungs were filled with water, but I was calm, at peace, and I knew I was dying.

All of the things people speak of when they have a near-death experience happened to me. I saw the tunnel...the white light...family on the other side, not in human form, but in light bodies.

That was not the first time I'd had a near-death experience. Each time my dad beat me unconscious, put a gun to my head, and I passed out, the same thing would happen to me. Each time I would say that I wanted to go back into my body, that I was not done in my Earth suit.

That near-death event was one I remember much clearer than the others. It was an act of God. I heard a voice as clear as day that told me that I needed to make a choice...to let go and surrender to the peace, or to return to my body. The voice continued to explain that coming back into my body would be extremely painful and frightening, but I would live. Or I could slip into the blissful embrace of the Divine, but I needed to choose, *immediately*. I said that I was not done in my Earth body and still had more to accomplish in this life. There was no judgment of my choice, just acceptance and love.

No sooner had I made that choice then I was thrust out of the water at such an incredible velocity that I must have looked like a pale, naked, dolphin flying through the air. The experience stripped any question from my mind that there is a God.

I scrambled to shore and walked back to town with only a tube wrapped around my naked body. I had no idea where the rest of our motley crew had floated off to, and cared about as much as I figured they cared about my whereabouts or well being. I was never the same after that experience.

CHAPTER 25

"Dear God...I'm fourteen years old. I've always been a good girl."
- Quote from The Color Purple

Soon after my near-drowning, my dad went back to Dallas and then on to Corpus Christi. He went back to his love of the sea and became a captain on an oil rig boat. We lost touch for several months. While I was dreaming those months would become years, I found out I was pregnant.

I was fourteen years old (the same age as Oprah, again parallel lives). I was blessed with a gift of life. A life that I wanted so desperately to love and hold and that would love me back, unconditionally. That was my dream, and I believed it would complete my mission in this life with this body.

Wes' grandmother let us live with her for a while, until she had enough of the pot smoking, jobless, good-for-nothings that we were. We were taking advantage of her caretaking nature and hospitality, eating her out of house and home. Her daughter, Curly, brought her enabling tendencies to her attention. I actually thought her daughter was a man until I walked into the bathroom one day and discovered Curly was really Colleen. That certainly changed the dynamics of my conversations with Curly-Colleen.

So, with the fortitude of Curly behind her, Nanny kicked us out. Off we went to my Uncle Steve and Aunt Kathy's in Colorado. They opened their home to us, and we were more than happy to find another couch and fridge to take advantage of until we were no longer welcome. I say "we" but I should say "he." Wes was a professional bum. I was embarrassed by that life, of not contributing to my own livelihood. Wes however, had made a life of couch hopping, burning relationships, and not working.

I was overjoyed to be with my family and to have a connection with them once again. I saw the look on their faces when they opened the door to see the spitting image of my dad by my side in Wes. How frightened they were for my choice in a mate. It didn't take any time at all before my aunt was fed up with all the highlighted want ads she left for Wes being lost in the smoke of his marijuana-induced laziness.

It was time for him to go. I could stay, but he was no longer welcome. Fearing for my life, I went with him. Did I mention he was also physically abusive? Oh. Well, yes, of course he was. We found an apartment and we probably stayed there less than two weeks before my life changed forever. Standing in the bathroom, water poured from my vagina onto the floor. I suddenly realized I was about to become a mother. A fourteen-year-old child with no mother was going to *be* a mother. Suddenly, doubts began running through my head as my water was running down my legs.

"Who is going to help me to know what to do?"

"What the hell do you do with a baby anyway?"

My brief experience of being forced to raise my infant sister when I was five years old was certainly no help. She nearly died from eating glass under my care. A shock wave went through me as I realized I hadn't thought the plan all the way through.

In my state of shock, I decided I needed to put my makeup on. I had to look good going to the hospital, after all. I let Wes know that my water broke and he immediately went into a full-blown panic. I was primping; he was panicking.

I never contemplated how my life was going to change forever once my child came into my life. I never really took the time to contemplate my life in general; there was too much drama to focus. I remembered in the past when I spent time in nature that I was able to slow my mind down in order to be in the now. But right NOW you are going to go to the hospital, and you are going to have a baby come out of your vagina, and it is going to hurt like hell. Then you are going to be responsible for the health and safety of a child. Oh shit!

A panicked dialog started running through my head.

"By society's standard, you are not old enough to take care of yourself."

"You have no education, no money. You have isolated yourself from the only family that loves you."

"Your father is insane, and the father of your child is your father's

twin flame..."

"Really, really, really look at this! Your life is going to be changed forever!"

And then I remembered why I was doing it; my child would be the one person that would love me truly, deeply, and unconditionally. My child had to love me....

As I write this now, I think back to this time in my life and realize how naïve I really was, as most teenage moms are. On our way to the hospital, I felt sadness within my heart because I had left my aunt and uncle's house on bad terms. And because of that, I wouldn't have them with me at the hospital. I was scared. I felt so alone within my relationship with Wes. Our "love" was all fire, no balance. We played off each other's victim mentality. We enabled each other's co-dependent, self-destructive behavior. We were a perfect mess.

Fear began building and building during the ride to the hospital. It was a huge energy ball of fear. By the time I made it to the hospital, I was very nauseated and shaking inside. Contractions started coming closer and closer together, and I started vomiting and could not stop. It was a combination of fear and pain that made me continue to vomit until I had nothing but bile to purge, but even then it did not stop.

I had a little girl, a beautiful little angel. I named her Ginger Nicole. She had big, beautiful blue eyes and long limbs. She was just perfect. I was so very sorry to have brought her into a world of pure fear. I was so filled with fear that there was no way for her not to feel that fear too.

When it was time to bring Ginger home, we had a home to bring her to because Wes actually had a job for the first time in our entire relationship. We had a nursery, and she had her very own crib. Well, at least for the first month of her life. Staying true to form, Wes lost his job, we lost the apartment, and we found ourselves living in a car.

Yes, we were living in a beat-up Chevy Vega with sleeping bags, a newborn baby drinking cold formula, and me, a fourteen-year-old mother praying that my child would live and that I would wake up from the nightmare of my life.

CHAPTER 26

"Surround yourself with only people
who are going to lift you higher."
- Oprah Winfrey

I don't remember how long we lived in the car before we met a couple that took us into their home. We lived in their spare bedroom as long as they would let us leech off of them, but soon we wore out our welcome. Even sympathy for a newborn baby was not enough to tolerate Wes' abusive, parasitic behavior. What an amazing couple to have shared their love with us as long as they did.

So we were on our way back to Texas to mooch off of his grandmother once again. His grandmother was the only enabler that would still enable us. We had burned all the other bridges with anyone else that cared enough to show us any charity. Wes was smart enough to realize that the situation with his grandmother was temporary, and much to my dismay, decided telling my father that he had become a grandfather might get us an extra handout.

My dad asked us to come to Corpus and said he would get Wes a job on the ship as a merchant seaman. We could all find a house together, and because my dad is on the boat most of the year, he really wouldn't even live there.

We had a baby and nowhere to live, so off we went. We bought a VW bug and put a crib mattress on the back seat for Ginger to sleep on during the journey to our new home. No car seat, no seatbelt, just a mattress. Thinking of that now just blows my mind, that I would lay my baby in the backseat on a mattress and think that it was safe. I don't even remember what the car seat rules were then, but I thought she had a cozy space for the trip.

Once we arrived in Corpus Christi, we had no idea that the "home" that my father was speaking of would start off in a hotel room. I'm not quite sure what I thought it would be, but it wasn't a hotel room. Seeing my father look at my daughter and then look at Wes made me feel like I had just brought alien beings to the Pope—just a bit uncomfortable to say the least.

My father attempted to bond with Ginger the best he could, but he had such a hard time with any type of intimacy. Of course he did not want intimacy with anyone in the sense of IN-TO-ME-SEE. That was something he rebelled against his entire life. When it came to the relationship between him and Wes, I watched them with this sinking, ill feeling within my gut, accompanied by that watery, metallic taste in my mouth. I again saw clearly that I had picked my father's clone in Wes, and here they were together, both with their egos seeking weakness in the guise of getting to know each other. There could be only one...

My goal was to get away from my father, from the hell of memories that were surrounding me on a daily basis: the abuse, the incest, the emptiness. How is it that I could have done that? What is it in my mind that attracts the precise thing that I so much want to rid myself of?

Wes soon started working on the oil rig boats, and he and my father would leave for two to three weeks at a time. I was left to stay with the wife of another oil rig worker, a complete stranger, who drank diet cokes, ate Spaghettios, and watched soap operas all day.

Soon after that, we claimed our new home...a double-wide trailer full of cockroaches. The cockroaches had no idea they were no longer on the lease, and held fast to their well-established turf. I was left alone with baby Ginger and the cockroaches. I really did not like being alone because I had no knowledge of who I was. But Ginger was the most perfect baby. They say God only gives you what you can handle, and she was perfection in the baby department. I was still such a baby in so many ways that I needed a baby sitter myself, but I was the best mother I knew how to be with the limited knowledge that I had at the ripe old age of fifteen. Ginger was born a week before my fifteenth birthday, and two hours late of being a Valentine baby. I loved her so much! She gave me such unconditional love, which was something I had never experienced before in my life.

I remember the first time she laughed. I was playing with one of those weebels, spinning it on the counter for her, and she giggled. I was so excited that I kept spinning it over and over, listening to that beautiful sound.

Late one night I started my period and had no tampons, so I decided I was going to drive to the store. Mind you, I had no driver's license and no driving experience, but it was just down the street. What harm could come? Plus, I was bored out of my mind and needed to see some other human being besides the characters on General Hospital.

I ran out of gas on an isolated road that seemed void of any living creatures, let alone a gas station. Suddenly I was very aware of the fight or flight feeling coming over me as a car pulled over and this very large man got out to assist me in ways that I was not at all comfortable with. He said he would go up the street and get me some gas. While I had my hand on the pistol my dad left under the seat, I thanked him and began praying to whomever and whatever might save me from what I knew were this man's intentions when he returned. Why he went to get the gas first was not clear, other than to make me feel safe before he raped me in the middle of nowhere with baby Ginger lying in the seat beside me.

My prayers were answered when the police pulled up beside me and waited for the man to return with the gas. They filled my car up and escorted me back to the trailer, then waited for quite a while to make sure the scary man did not follow us back.

Not long after that, my father and Wes came home for a two-week leave at the same time. They wanted to party, and I wanted to join them, but we did not have a babysitter. So we made an agreement. Wes would be responsible, and I would have the fun. I didn't really drink alcohol anymore since Ginger's birth, but it was there, and I decided that I had been locked up in that trailer for way too long and I deserved to let loose. And did I ever!

We jumped into the Volkswagen, baby and all, and went to the beach. I got plastered. I realized I had hit a wall when instead of putting the beer bottle to my mouth, I put Ginger's bottle in my mouth. When we arrived home, I wanted to pass out. Or should I say, I was passing out, want to or not. I remember my dad and Wes putting me and baby Ginger in the bedroom and walking towards the door.

On the way down I said, *"Please do not leave me here with the baby and go back out, I can't take care of her!"*

The next thing I remember is hearing the sound of the car starting. When I realized that they were going to keep partying and leave me alone with her, I flew into a rage. Literally flew. I was so angry I became airborne as I catapulted for the window. I think I intended to jump right through it and grab them out of the car, but the laws of physics, along with the metal bars over the window, had other ideas.

I crashed through the glass, hit the bars, and was violently bounced back onto the bed. The sturdy metal bars saved me from going all the way through the glass and being cut to ribbons, but instead I cut my leg open and threw shattered glass all over the baby that Wes left lying next to me. Thank God she was unhurt, just terrified and screaming.

Hearing the glass break, the thud of me hitting the bars, and the screaming baby, my dad and Wes came running back inside to see what had happened. But it was no rescue effort. My father proceeded to beat me and slap me across the face repeatedly. First, because I was so out of control mad that I did not realize that I was bleeding a puddle on the carpet. Understand that their concern was not for my well-being—I was ruining the fucking carpet! And I broke the window (So much for the property value of Chez Dirtbag)! And second, because he was so pissed that I had interrupted their partying.

How could they leave me with that baby when I could not even take care of myself? The answer is simple, when people are engaged in active addiction there is nothing more important than getting high or drunk.

CHAPTER 27

"Understand that the right to choose your own path is a sacred privilege. Use it. Dwell in possibility."
- Oprah Winfrey

Sometime after that, we ended up moving to our new home, which was a trailer that you would normally see at a construction site. Living next door was the cutest girl; she was my age and was very nice to me when we moved in. I can't explain the feeling that came over me to have someone to connect with when I was alone with the baby for weeks at a time. I wanted a friend, someone to talk to...someone to love. And I did, I fell in love with her on every level. I was so desperate to fill the void within my heart that gender did not matter. I just wanted to be wanted and filled up. She did that for me. We became very close, she took me shopping, we went to the beach, we laughed, we made love, we held each other, and we were connected.

Wes came home for his two-week stay and discovered the gifts that Lori had bought me. He thought they were from another man. No matter what I said, he thought I had taken a male lover. I told him that it was a woman and she no threat to him. He asked me to prove it to him and bring her over. So I did, very apprehensively, and for good reason.

He forced us into performing sexual acts with each other for him, and then he forced himself on her. I was so filled with rage and pain when I looked in her eyes. I saw the resentment and anguish that was mine when I had been forced to do sexual acts in my past.

She left my home and she left my heart. She was no longer available to be my friend. I would cry each and every time I would look out the window and see her face. There was a level of hate inside of me toward Wes that would never be removed after that incident. I was once again alone with the baby, and oh so very bored.

Before long, Wes and my dad were home, once again on the same schedule, and decided to go to the local bar. Dad had a brilliant plan to make extra money. He had bought a large quantity of hashish and wanted Wes to sell it at the bar and pay the rent with the money he received. Dad was very specific in instructing Wes not to give him any of the money that he made because he knew he would spend it.

The wait at the trailer was a long one for me that night. It was getting later and later, and we did not have a phone to connect with each other. For all I knew they could be in jail, or beating the crap out of each other or someone else that got in their way. My dad and Wes had discovered that they were exactly alike too, and their egos were bigger than the local Super Walmart.

I heard a thud at the door, not really a knock, but a noise that appeared to be someone attempting to knock. By then I was filled with anger. I knew that it was one of them, drunk and falling down, and I would have to deal with their belligerent, obnoxious, self righteous, demeanor. I opened the door and almost threw up and passed out at the same time.

Wes was standing at the door and his throat was cut open. The majority of his neck was filleted open and lying on his chest. He was cut from ear to chin, and blood was pouring from him and soaking his clothes. I rushed him to the emergency room and they said that he was lucky to be alive. It had missed his carotid artery by a hair. Once he came back to consciousness, I asked him what had happened.

"Your dad wanted the money he told me to hold onto. It was our agreement and I held him to that. He was so drunk and full of rage with me that he pulled his gun from his boot and tried to shoot me, but it wouldn't go off. So he pulled his knife and cut my throat. He's in jail and it's amazing that I'm still alive. Aleta, I can't live with your father, he is completely out of his mind."

I could not believe that my own father had attempted to kill the father of my child. He had gone too far. I went to visit my father at the local jail to let him know how I felt. When I saw him sitting there, I saw a man that was drained of any life force. His spirit was gone and there was only a shell of a body there. He was alive, but not in the sense of doing anything other than breathing. He had lost his will to live, just as his mother had when my grandfather died.

I asked him, *"Dad, why? I don't understand, you asked him to hold the money!"*

He said nothing.

We looked at each other and somehow there was an unspoken agreement that we were done. Maybe it was the bars that separated us, maybe I had finally reached the breaking point, but I laid down the law.

I spoke from a place of power, calmly and without anger, *"You know what? It doesn't even matter. I don't care what your reason is. There is no reason that could justify what you've done. You're sick. You have to leave, and I don't ever want to see you again. I am not pressing charges. I want you to come and get your things from the house, and I want you to leave the state. Don't ever call me or contact me in any way ever again."*

I don't know what shifted, but he actually complied. When he was released, he returned to the trailer and gathered his things. He remained detached and silent, almost zombie-like. If I didn't know any better, I would almost say he was remorseful.

I packed him some sandwiches and walked him to the car. I knew in my heart that I would never see him again. Believe it or not, there was actually an element of sadness between whatever remnants were left of father and daughter, and we both felt it. We hugged and said goodbye. I watched him drive away in his old Ford Fairlane and said, *"Good bye, daddy. I wish you could have known who I was and loved me. Better yet, I wish you could have known and loved yourself."*

When Wes was released from the hospital, only three of us comprised our little dysfunctional family: Wes, Ginger, and me. We continued on with our life without my father.

One night, Wes and I decided to go to a concert. We got a sitter and went out, and I realized how long it had been since we had a date. Really, I don't know why I thought it would be a fun thing to do, because anything that involved alcohol with Wes turned me into a punching bag, and that was not my idea of date night. But I was so excited to get out and have some time to be me. Not just a mom, sitting at home, being a mom. That night the drinking began before we even arrived at the concert, but everything appeared to be going in a good direction. We were having fun until the drummer of the band waved me over to the stage. I immediately told Wes and asked for him to come with me. I think that his selective "man hearing" was turned on and I was not aware of the punch coming toward my face until it was too late. I remember feeling so incredibly ashamed and humiliated in front of the entire stadium of people and the band.

I thought: *I am getting punched in the face by the father of my child.*

I ran, and I ran, and I ran, until I realized I was in the parking lot and there was nowhere for me to go. How many times had I felt that way in my life after getting a beating? Running and realizing that I was going to have to turn around and crawl back to the place of pain, both external and internal. I knew nothing of battered women's shelters at that time, nor did I feel that I could contact my aunt and uncle after the way we left their home that cold night in Colorado. I was observing myself as I ran around the parking lot watching all of the people pretend that I was not in danger from a drunken man who obviously wanted to beat me.

Those people did nothing. The security did nothing. I was puzzled that there was no one willing to take action.

I finally caved to my lack of options and submissively got in the car with Wes. The night was different in that I felt a separation from him, as well as a churning of anger that seemed final. Perhaps taking my power with my father had fortified me for that night. I was sitting in the back seat of the car as he drove in a quiet rage to a remote wooded area. He pulled over and launched into the back seat with a vicious attack, beating me with what I soon realized was the intent to kill me. Fight or flight kicked in, and it was going to be a real fight. I was not going down! Not at the hands of that son of a bitch in the backseat of a Volkswagen in the woods. I had a life to live, and I had a purpose in this world, so I fought. I blacked out in rage, and after kicking him over and over in the face, he finally stopped.

We drove home in silence. When we woke the next morning, I had large golfball-sized knots on my head and several broken ribs. Wes usually didn't hit my face; he would choke me with coat hangers, hit me in the head, hit me in the ribs, kick me, but rarely touched my face. I am sure that made it easier for him to live with his insanity, because he really couldn't see what he had done physically and he would ignore my moaning as I attempted to pick up my baby and feed her.

Life for me in that toxic relationship really wasn't living. I barely existed. In moments of rebellion, I would pack up the baby and my clothes and start to walk down the street, then stop and ask myself:

"Where do you think you are going?"
And then I would return to the misery that was my home.

There have been so many apologies that I have made to Ginger over the years for not giving her up for adoption and for letting her grow up in such a hellish environment. I know that environment changed her to her soul. She has never felt safe in this world, and to this day it makes me cry that she still doesn't.

CHAPTER 28

"Where there is no struggle, there is no strength."
- Oprah Winfrey

A knock on the door from the police is not what you want or expect when you are home alone smoking pot. I'm not sure what I was prepared for when I opened that door, but I was not prepared for what came next.

"We are here to let you know that your father is in critical condition in a New Orleans hospital. You need to call him ASAP."

My heart dropped, and my feelings were of sadness and relief simultaneously. It was a dichotomy because I was sad that he was hurt, but excited that he might die. I attempted to call and speak to him, but divine intervention never allowed the timing for that to happen. After three days of trying, I finally got hold of a nurse who told me that an hour before my call, my father had passed away.

"What happened? What was his cause of death?"

After a medical description that was incomprehensible to my heart or mind, she shared the circumstances she had heard from the police. My father was at a seedy bar on the dirty side of New Orleans and he had thousands of dollars on him. He had just cashed his check after docking his ship. He was being cocky, confrontational, and belligerent while flashing his cash around. That was his usual M.O. He pissed off several people and was beat so badly that most people with good health wouldn't have survived. But with a whiskey soaked liver, lungs filled with smoke, and God knows what other chemicals that were poisoning his system, he had no chance.

For some reason I felt obligated to do something, at least to honor the part of him that was once my father, so I called Steve and Kathy.

"Uncle Steve, Dad died. I don't have any money for a funeral, or

even a casket. Can you please help?"

I was so raw and helpless at fifteen years old. I could not feel anything but anger and abandonment at the resounding "NO" that answered my request.

I had to allow the city of New Orleans to bury my father. I did not get to have closure, and for many years I saw my father everywhere I turned—in the store, on the street, in the bathroom. It was all illusion, of course.

CHAPTER 29

"I believe we are still so innocent. The species are still so innocent that a person who is apt to be murdered believes that the murderer, just before he puts the final wrench on his throat, will have enough compassion to give him one sweet cup of water."
- Maya Angelou

We packed up and headed back to Dallas. I left behind my friend Lori and the construction site trailer, knowing that I would never see my father again. We were going back to Wes' grandmother's house. She was someone we always fell back on for support. She always gave in, and then held resentments.

The lesson I learned from Nanny is that a true gift is given from the heart with nothing wanted or expected in return, not even a thank you. I learned from Nanny what can happen when you enable your children and then continue to enable them into their twenties and thirties. In my mind, it is a form of child abuse. Looking back at all that Nanny did for us, I am truly grateful. I only wish that she had given Wes and his brother the gift of love so that they would have grown into healthy men instead of staying dysfunctional, angry boys. Nanny was an amazing, loving woman with a heart of gold. I miss her. She was and is Ginger's angel.

However, being the mother of an infant and having no way of earning a living, I was grateful she continued to enable us both so that we could eat and have a roof over our heads, even if that gift came with strong undertones of resentment each time she walked in the room. People don't have to speak for you to know their energy is not conducive with what their façade is portraying.

There is a song by John Mellencamp that includes the verse: *"the bed's made but there is no sheets on"*. This verse always resonated with me when I met people that were not what their mask portrayed on the outside.

The abuse, the lack of a job, the drugs, and having no home of our own was beginning to weigh on me in a way that can only be described as a heavy cloud of shame that followed me wherever I went. Wes came home drunk from a topless bar one afternoon and threw me down on the floor in the bedroom. He shoved his dick in my mouth and held me there. There is always a breaking point in which you just can't take anymore, and that was it for me. I could not breathe and I could not take any more, so I bit down as hard as I could to get him off of me. He punched me in the face until I let go, then he flew off of me in a state of shock and pain. I ran out of the bedroom and realized that I had to get out of there. I had no one that I could call except my aunt and uncle, and that call would only come when I knew I was ready to leave, otherwise there was no point in telling them what I had been through. Why complain to someone if you're not going to take action to get yourself out of the situation?

When Wes left for work later that day, I called and told them everything. The beatings, the choking, the rapes, I told them everything that had happened with my father and Wes. I begged for them to please help get my baby girl and me out of there.

I had no idea that they would act so quickly and without hesitation. That was love expressed in the most beautiful form. Our plan was to meet my aunt at the park down the street from the house at a certain time. The key was to do it when Wes and Nanny were gone, but I never knew when that would be. So I had to just pick a time and pray that they would be gone. Just as I was about to walk out the door, Wes came in the house. I shoved the suitcase under the bed.

He said, *"I came home to get a quickie and a quick bite."*

I thought I was going to have a heart attack or throw up. I could not say no to him. That would only cause a fight, and then I would waste time to leave and meet my aunt. I knew she was down the block, and I had to make it happen. I had to escape.

So our goodbye was having sick sex before I watched him leave.

"Goodbye you complete jerk. I bid you a fond farewell, and as sick as it sounds, I love you and will miss you."

I dragged my suitcase and my daughter down the road, to the park, and into the loving arms of my aunt, who took us to a hotel and bought us lunch. I was so scared. I thought that he followed us and he was going to kill us all. It took me months to get over the fear of him finding us, even though we were in Colorado and he had no idea where we were.

Shortly after, I found myself walking through the halls of a high school with my aunt, on my way to take the test for my G.E.D. I was seventeen and ready for the test, but I had an aching in my heart to go back to school...to be a teenager...a normal teenager. I asked my aunt if she thought that could be an option for me instead of getting a G.E.D., and she said yes. It was a scary time, but it was also a heart-racing, exhilarating time.

I tested to see what grade they would place me in because of my lack of formal education, but I tested high and was able to go in as a sophomore. It was so exciting to go clothes shopping. I was unsure of how I was going to dress, where I wanted to place myself in the social "clicks" that are common in schools. I really felt that I did not belong anywhere. For one thing, I had a child, and for another, I had not been to school in years. I had no sense of identity other than a mother and a victim. I chose to go the prep route because that is what my new family seemed to be wearing and it seemed safe. I kept my secret life of being a mother from most of my classmates, except for my few closest friends that I developed after starting school.

I felt so free, so content in that new life, so normal. I watched my daughter grow as I grew into something different beside her. My family was very supportive, and I felt loved and safe. There was a part of me that felt like that was going to end soon, because I was so used to drama and pain.

I had become quite fond of a boy, and was getting very close to him. For the first time in my life, I was loved by a man without having to have sex with him. He adored me, and every day we would eat lunch together under a tree just talk. I felt too shy to eat in front of him, but I would watch him eat and then go home and stuff my face. He knew about my daughter and did not judge me. He just smiled when he saw Ginger and me together.

Then he asked me to prom. It was my dream to be able to wear a beautiful dress and be a princess for one evening. For some reason I thought my aunt would not buy me the dress that I wanted, although I don't know that she ever actually said that. The truth is, I was so used to my life being so bad that I didn't know how to handle it being so good. So, I acted out. I got so mad at the 'idea' that she wouldn't buy me the dress that I went across the street to my best friend's house and asked her mom to buy it for me. I told my aunt I was moving in with them. Looking back at this, I realize how immature I was in so many ways.

I don't remember how long I stayed with them before I returned home, but upon my arrival I was given the option by my family to either give up Ginger for adoption and go to school full-time like a "normal" teenager, or to be a mom and get a job. Why?!? Why would I have to choose?

I now know that I was not spending enough time with Ginger as a mother. It was not fair to her, and it was confusing her. But at the time I felt like it was unfair to me. I was being victimized again. Everything seemed fine, why were they doing this to me? Well, what did Aleta do when confronted with a situation that she didn't like?

RUN, RUN, RUN!

CHAPTER 30

"History, despite its wrenching pain, cannot be unlived,
but if faced with courage, need not be lived again."
- Maya Angelou

In a fit of hysteria, I absolutely lost my mind and called Wes in Texas and told him we were coming home. Somehow I thought that would really show my aunt and uncle.

I'll show you for caring about my daughter and me! I will pack our stuff, sneak out of the house in the middle of the night, take a cab to the airport, and go back to my abuser for a fun-filled life of beatings, poverty, drug addiction, regret, and shame for making that choice. I'll show you!

I remember getting off the plane and walking toward a man that no longer appealed to me in any way. There was Wes, a biker with tattoos and a trashy, beat-up car with gunshot holes in the windows. There I was, wearing my Izod sweater, with my daughter in her beautiful dress and black patent leather shoes, looking up at me with a face that seemed to say, *"Have you lost your fucking mind?!?!?!"*

Yes. Oh, yes I had. And what better way to push that down than to start getting high as soon as possible.

Wes wanted to get married so we wouldn't have another child out of wedlock. I was so incredibly scared of him after all of the beatings I had taken from him that I agreed. We got married in his aunt's house, and I thought I could just puke. That was not the man God chose for me, that was not what marriage was meant to be, something forced, something made in fear—not love—but I did it, out of fear of another beating.

Although, what later came of that decision turned out to be one of the greatest gifts of my life. I planned and gave birth to my second beautiful daughter, Amber. I know that within the curse of my decision there was a gift, thank God.

Amber was a healthy baby, and a big eight pounds, four ounces. She was perfect and she was happy. I didn't throw up the whole time while giving birth. Amber was not born into fear like Ginger, and her life is now a reflection of that.

Wes continued our life as if we never parted. The drama, pain, beatings, and drug addiction continued. I became addicted to meth and cocaine for a while, but I never did drugs around my children. I would let Nanny baby-sit and then get high at someone else's house.

I remember the day I realized that I was being consumed by the evil chemicals. I sat in my car in the driveway of my dealer with my newborn daughter for four hours, waiting for him to come home. I just wanted the hookup, and then I would drop my daughter off with Nanny and her sister and go party.

On some level I knew that my life was destined for more. I knew that there was greatness within me, a Divine spark that had allowed me to make it thus far. After all that I had been through, I *was not* on the path to the life I was meant to lead. That path was a blasphemy to my true life, a denial of it, and a path to more pain, suffering, and death. I looked down at my beautiful baby, who still held that Divine spark, and I knew I was done.

I quit cold turkey. Sometime after that, I became very good friends with a woman who was a dental hygienist. I was fascinated with her because she smoked pot and was able to complete very difficult schooling. She made incredible money in an environment that I had never experienced. I picked her brain constantly about her field; I wanted so badly to have a career. I did not want to continue working at grocery stores.

One day, she came to me with great news. The dentist she worked for was hiring a dental assistant, she told him about me, and he said he would be willing to train me. I was ecstatic! It was my chance to make something of my life.

The first thing that Wes said was, *"You're going to meet a dentist and leave me."*

I appeased him and said, *"Oh, no, honey. I would not do that."*

Oh, hell yes I would! Get me there and let me make it happen! It was the key to my escape from of the hellhole of my own creation.

CHAPTER 31

"What God intended for you goes
far beyond anything you can imagine."
- Oprah Winfrey

I started working at the dental office and my world changed. I was surrounded by people that lived in a completely different paradigm. I am a very fast learner, and felt as though I was always meant to be in that field. I developed self-esteem, and I was so proud to work there. I learned so much from the different women that surrounded me. I worked with one dentist most of the time and had many dumb blond moments (or as I now like to call them "Lucy moments" in tribute to Lucille Ball).

Once, I was developing an x-ray and I was wearing a cloth belt that wrapped around my scrubs. Somehow, the end of the belt got caught in the x-ray machine. I was in the dark, getting pulled towards the machine, and I was scared but laughing at the same time.

Another morning, the doctor was knocking on the back door so I attempted to let him in by turning the key from the inside, but it broke off in the lock. I ran and hid. I certainly did not want him to know that I was the one that kept him locked out of his own office for more than an hour.

I was learning to place brackets (braces), but I was not taught everything. One important step was missing: etching. Etching prepares the enamel for the adhesive and bonding. Without that step, the brackets won't adhere. I spent an hour and a half putting on a full set of brackets with this poor patient's mouth held open, and as soon as they got up all of them fell off. Live (hopefully laugh) and learn. I did all of the above.

Wes was the stay at home dad and I was the provider. I loved getting away from him whenever I could. He would drive me to work every day in a full-blown road rage so I could start my day with a big steaming cup of fear. But once I shook it off and went into my new identity, I was free.

I worked with one dentist named Brad that came in once a week to do root canals. He was gorgeous and so perfect; perfectly unavailable, and perfectly married. Right...perfect. We flirted, and I knew that I wanted him, no matter the circumstances. I wasn't particularly good at understanding or respecting boundaries, since I had never been allowed to have any.

He was married and miserable and so was I. What better combination could there be to begin an affair to remember? He made me feel sexy and wanted, and I made him feel young. The sex was incredible because it was so wrong and sneaky, and that made it amazing.

It went on for many months. I began to look at my home life with distain, and threw up every time Wes would rape me. Yes, husbands can rape their wives. The beatings were getting more frequent, and it was destroying my children. Mostly, it affected my oldest, Ginger, who was six and old enough to know that mommy was not okay when she screamed.

I remember seeing her peep out of her door and cry as she watched him hit me. She closed the door, and seeing her pain filled me with so much rage that radiated throughout my body that I picked up an iron and hit him over the head. I just knew I had killed him, and I was going to go to prison like all the other women who were serving time for self-defense from abusive mates.

He lived, but I died when I looked into the mirror and saw an old woman with a closed heart. I was only twenty years old. That was it, if I stayed any longer one of us was really going to die.

I asked Brad, my dentist lover, to help me move out. He hired several large bouncer/movers to move us to our new one-bedroom apartment. I had a bed in the living room for myself and the girls had two cots in the bedroom, but we were happy and we were free of Wes and all the pain he caused us. Well, almost free. Wes continued stalking me for some time.

I realized I would never be free of him and the hell that followed unless I took drastic action, so I filed for divorce. That might not seem drastic to you, but to a girl who had been a victim stuck in the same pattern of being a doormat to abusive men her whole life, it was huge. It was the first step to regaining my power. But getting him to sign the papers was impossible. Funny, he never stalked me when I had those papers in my hand.

Finally, I was forced to go to a crackhouse to corner him into signing. That was a very scary thing for me, it felt like walking back into the gates of hell. I almost expected Cerberus to greet me at the door. I also expected a war with Wes, but surprisingly, neither happened. He actually signed with no problems. I don't know if that was an act of concession, or momentary pacifism due to the drugs coursing through his veins, but I wasn't sticking around to find out. I took the papers and ran.

After less than two years of marriage—or rather prison with beatings and rape by my so-called husband—the papers were signed, and I walked out of prison and never looked back.

I was at a loss of what to do with myself without all of the drama and pain, so I began coaching Ginger's soccer team to keep myself busy. That helped me from doing crazy things, like attempting to call Wes, my beloved abuser. I have no idea why I would want to do that; it was just a pattern, a sick pattern ingrained in me from my childhood. Love me, hit me, love me, hurt me, love me, hate me…God, can't somebody just love me?

After the divorce was finalized, I continued the affair with Brad until one Christmas when he and I went to the mall after one of our carnal lunchtime meetings.

When we pulled up he said, *"Wait here, I will be back."*

As I sat in the car, I thought, *"How sweet, he is going to buy me a gift!"*

I was so happy. He came back with the gift…for his wife. At that moment, I realized my delusion of believing that he would ever leave her or love me enough was over. I admitted to myself that it would never be anything more to him than a good fuck with a younger girl on the side. So, my gift to myself was to make him go away, and I did.

Merry Christmas to me.

CHAPTER 32

*"I long, as does every human being,
to be at home wherever I find myself."
- Maya Angelou*

After the Christmas awakening I had with Brad, I decided it would be best to move to a new city to start a new life. I blew off Brad, quit my job, moved to Garland, Texas, and got a new job with a new dentist named Bill.

Bill had a pool party at his house and invited my daughters and me to come. The girls and I were in the pool with the others, when he walked over and bent down next to the pool to connect with the girls. Then he said he had to run to watch his daughter play soccer.

I automatically thought, *"Family man, nice house, dentist...provider for my girls! And this one's not even married!"*

When it got late and the party started clearing out, I went to work using my sexual power to lure him in with actions like very sexually bending over at the fridge to get a beer. I did anything I could to snag him. I put the girls to bed in his bed upstairs because I had a mission—him. I was horny, and my radar was going off that he could be a man that could help me take care of my girls. For me, at that time, it was all about survival.

When he offered me a joint, I thought, *"OMG this guy has it all!"*
WRONG!

Although he was not married, he was not available emotionally. He couldn't even give a hug. So, of course, I decided I could fix him! I put on my superhero cape and assigned myself the duty of breaking through his shell of pain to show him that he could love me. I was going to save the day! Hello? Aleta? Why are you unable to discern between a red flag and BIG freakin' red flag?!?

If someone does not even feel comfortable getting hugged, and is so introverted you have to use a crowbar to engage him in a conversation, coupled with an energy that radiated depression, and that could be a BIG red flag that he is unavailable. HERE'S YOUR SIGN! Oh, but my 'pain body' loved unavailable men. That made me feel comfortable and at home with that warm, fuzzy feeling inside. I would continue to try and make an intimate relationship work with someone who would rather not have IN-TO-ME-SEE with anyone.

But, put a couple of horny, lonely pain bodies together with some alcohol and weed, and the party is pumping! I become so sad thinking about how desperate and unconscious I was back then, but I was only twenty-one years old and lost.

I went to check on the girls upstairs, so he followed me up. I thought he was being kind, but he was really just horny. All of my seductive entrapments brought to fruition. He began fondling me. I thought the girls could not see what was going on because he was doing it below eye-level of the bed, but Ginger told me later that she hated him from that day on!

To this day, I feel shame and guilt that I allowed that to happen in front of my children. Again, I thought they couldn't see it, but I never should have even exposed them to it. I'm sure drugs, alcohol, and being twenty-one and lost had a lot to do with my poor decision making in that moment. I still have to work on forgiving myself for that one.

At least I had secured a new relationship and security for my children. And we were happy, happy, happy...for as long as we could pretend to be. At first, my ego was dancing! I was dating a dentist! I did not have to hide the relationship from the wife because this one was divorced! Or so I thought.

After dating for several months and moving most of my things into his home, a woman calls one day and says, *"Who's this?"*

I, of course, am thinking the real question is, *"Who the hell is this?"*

She said, *"This is Linda. I am his wife."*

Houston, we have a problem!

His wife? Doesn't that just warm your cockles? (What are cockles anyway, and why do we want to warm them?)

"Well, Linda, I'll be sure to let him know that you called, okay? Buh-bye now."

I knew I had a good thing going there. Okay, from that perspective it seemed good. I mean, I was already moved in. So, rather than reaching for the nearest iron, I calmly asked him who "Linda" was. He said that she had packed up and moved out when he was at work, took everything, moved to Hawaii, and he could not find her to divorce her.

That could have been something you shared with me before I moved in. Once I have my children's Nintendo and most of my belongings in your house, it means we're kind of serious.

They finally divorced around the time I realized that my inner pain addict loved that relationship and wanted to make sure that I was sufficiently fixed up on the drama department for the next decade or so. Somehow, I thought my world was going to be perfect from then on.

We didn't marry right away, but we moved into a beautiful home with a pool. I did not have to worry about how I would take care of my daughters any longer. Our housing was paid for, and all I had to do was cover the girl's expenses and we were golden.

Of course, the newness wore off pretty quick. We took down the masks of perfection and non-realistic behavior and the feeding began. I remember one day his daughter, Skyla, came to visit. At least he had mentioned her, so I wasn't caught completely off-guard again. We were going to have our Disneyland daddy weekend. That was when we did everything fun because it was her weekend to visit.

My kids were thinking, *"Who the hell is she to get this treatment? What's wrong with us?"*

I had this beautiful fedora hat that I adored, and when we all got in the car to go for a road trip, I put it on the floorboard in the backseat, which was probably a mistake since the whole car was filled with kids and the trunk was filled with stuff.

I said to the kids, *"This is mommy's new hat. Please, please do not put your feet on this side."*

We make our first stop at a gas station and I looked down to a squashed hat and a manipulative stepdaughter grin. I thought, *"What have I gotten myself and my children into?"*

I attempted the path of peace, trying everything to connect with her, but she was unavailable to my intentions. I soon discovered that she was often hurt by her mother, who was a major alcoholic and never thought that Skyla was good enough. Her mother somehow missed the fact that Skyla was a genius and excelled at anything she did.

I also found out that her daddy just divorced wife number five, so I knew that child was not feeling safe or loved, and she saw me as just another temporary fixture that took her daddy's attention from her.

I tried putting makeup on her just to connect with her and show her how.

She looked up at me and said, *"If I don't like you, I will make you leave just like I have with all the others."*

I said, *"Honey you have no idea who you're dealing with. You can't make me go anywhere."*

She was respectful from then on, at least to my face. She just did things behind our backs and lied. I tried to treat her with the love that she was missing, but I was so full of jealousy when it came to her. I couldn't explain it. Instead of making her feel like part of the family when she came over, she got special treatment, and that made me angry.

Bill and I continued to work together and things got more drama-filled by the minute. I remember wanting to just blow up at him, but this little voice would say, *"Don't do it, he will leave you. Don't push him away."* I had no clue how to communicate or even feel my feelings. If I couldn't be real with myself, then how could I be real in any relationship?

CHAPTER 33

"I've learned that people will forget what you said; people will forget what you did, but people will never forget how you made them feel."
- Maya Angelou

Four years after moving in together, Bill and I married. I told him before I accepted his proposal that I wanted another child. He assured me we would, but in the end, he never gave me one. It was a primary contention between us. I look back on it now and am grateful we did not have a child together, by the grace of God go I. Ginger was about ten and Amber was six, and it was around that time that Ginger quit talking all together. She had started shutting down more and more after we moved in. Several incidents had happened, from seeing me being beaten by Wes, to the fondling by Bill, to what I now suspect (but cannot prove) was her own sexual abuse. It hurt her psyche and she just pulled further and further away.

It was then that I began my crusade to find out what was wrong with my daughter, when all along I should have been working on what was wrong with me. Focusing on the problems of another is a wonderful distraction to keep you from having to deal with your own. I sent her to numerous therapists that she would get close to, and for some reason they would quit or leave. Understandably, this did nothing to make her feel safe and just contributed to more abandonment issues for her, which finally made her not want to work with any therapist.

One therapist named Pat came out of a session and said, *"Your daughter just sits and stares at the clock. You would be better off coming in her spot and getting your money's worth."*

I realized she was right. And so, I began the journey of my own healing once again. I had done some therapy when I lived with my aunt and uncle, but that therapist was different. She really, truly cared about me. She was present, she was motherly, and I felt safe.

We made some amazing breakthroughs, and she was the first person that I wrote a poem for. It was a very child-like poem for a twenty-seven-year-old woman, but it was a child's creativity, for I had never tapped into my creative side. It was newly born. After reading it she said I had writing talent, and from just that one moment of someone believing in me, I began to believe in myself.

Pat suggested I quit smoking pot and go to meetings. She asked me to pack all my pipes, bongs, etc., and bring them to her to let her remove them from my life. So I did, and off I went to my first NA meeting. I felt scared and alone within the crowd of victims and pain bodies, but I trusted her and trudged through her suggestion with stubborn opposition.

I found a sponsor, worked through the steps a bit at a time, and brought all of the pain up from the past in the order that the steps recommended. I did not like it, but pain is pain for a reason...it hurts. Sometimes it made me feel sick as it came up, but I knew if I didn't deal with it that it would make me sick on the inside, and spread its poison and creating disease, or dis-ease.

Bill and I bought some land and decided to start building our dream home. It was actually fun! I had never been able to design something and watch it materialize into something so gorgeous! Our land was on top of a hill on Bluebonnet Lane in Palmer, Texas. People from all over Texas took tour buses to this street to see the bluebonnets. I loved that land, and I loved the thought of building a home and a family on that land.

Everything about it was perfect, except that I was still miserable in my own skin. I had not discovered who I was, or who I was capable of being. I was still discovering my spirituality, or lack thereof. I had gone through my "church stage," my "12 Step Stage," my "I don't like either of those choices" stage, and was then in the "What the hell does any of this mean?" stage.

CHAPTER 34

*"What I know is, if you do work that you love,
and the work fulfills you, the rest will come."*
- Oprah Winfrey

Bill and I began looking into the amalgam fillings we were putting into patients teeth, especially the possible negative effects it could create. Mercury fillings suddenly did not resonate with us at all. That led us to seek understanding of the toxicity in mercury-amalgam fillings (these are placed in everyone's teeth at a very young age), and other things like the nickel in crowns. We decided to attend a seminar on the subject given by a German healer, Dr. Dietrich Klinghardt.

The moment I walked into the room, I connected with Dr. Klinghardt on a level that had to have been based on past lives together. You know that feeling where there is instant strong energy flowing between you and a perfect stranger?

I 'knew' him and he 'knew' me, and that would turn into a friendship that is still present today, sixteen years later. The night of the seminar, as I laid my head down to sleep, I knew my whole world had just shifted. I was so grateful for that change. I had a dream about that beautiful German soul; he was in a restaurant and all of these women came up to him and called him by a different name.

The next morning I went to him and told him of the dream, and boy, if you could have seen the expression on his face.

He said, *"You know me, you really do. I have never been able to deal with all of the women I have brought into my life. I have been trying to change myself to be what I thought they wanted and have forgotten who I am."*

That was it for us. I thought I fell in love, and I had...I just did not understand what kind of love. I automatically thought that it was romantic love, and in my mind I spent years in his arms. He was my dream relationship, he was my spiritual man that was grounded, and he had something I wanted, which was a divine light within him that I had not seen in myself for a very long time.

Dietrich did so many different forms of healing, everything from neural therapy to emotional healing and color therapy. I was fascinated and I wanted what he had, all of it. I loved his laugh, his nonchalant attitude, as he would lick his butter knife in an inappropriate manner. I swooned over that man and his energy. The day I met Dietrich, my husband Bill was no longer good enough, and during the years to come he only got worse in my eyes. I compared him, judged him, and emasculated him with my poisonous words.

You can have an affair of the heart, you can have a sexual affair, and then you can have an affair of the mind that causes an instant disconnection with your spouse. That is what I did when I met Dietrich; I disconnected from my husband. I knew then and there that I wanted more and that I deserved it, but I was too afraid to leave the marriage for seven more years.

Bill and I continued to live in our beautiful house and we raised our beautiful kids. Well, we raised one: Amber. Ginger continued to run away, and she was in and out of rehabs, mental facilities, and the streets.

In my mind, I had my reasons for staying in an indifferent marriage. The primary reason was that I wanted my daughter Amber to have a stable homelife for once. I also wanted the financial security, and I wanted to stay until I grew my wings strong enough to fly out on my own and not fall on my face. Time was what I needed, and that is what I chose. I do not regret the choice of staying so long, but I regret the pain that I inflicted on that man with a broken heart, the man I took vows to love, honor, and cherish till death do us part.

How can someone make that commitment when one does not even know whom they are? How can we guarantee that we will not grow into something else, into someone else? What happens if our vibrations no longer match? I was so young when we met. We were together for fourteen years and married for ten. During that time, I don't know where the two of us went. We would sit in the same room, sleep in the same bed, but I would still feel completely alone...how was that possible? If he coughed, it irritated me. If he spoke, I wanted to hit him. I was jealous of the dogs, they got more attention and love than I did. I resented him for everything that he was and everything that he wasn't. There was no communication, and that was the primary reason we deteriorated and built up resentments over time that lead to a bitter, lonely, sexless marriage.

In the beginning we connected over dysfunction, drugs, and alcohol. When I quit and he didn't, it created an even larger gap between us called "nothing in common." I wanted him to be more of a man, but I castrated his testes years ago, and then wondered what happened to the man that I created in my mind. Where was his power? I wanted to change him into what I wanted, but I did not know what I wanted. What I wanted was constantly changing as I grew spiritually. I grew, while he stayed stagnant and depressed. What a convoluted state.

I remember reading this line in a book: "There is nothing worse than a marriage of indifference."

I had never been able to put into words what I was feeling, but that really nailed it for me. He was controlling, and do I mean *controlling*. I had a husband that made over six figures a year, but I had no access to any of the money. The only money I had was what I made working for him. I used that money to pay for our groceries and anything that had to do with Amber. I had no access to *his* bank account. There was no *ours*. I had no credit cards and I was broke most of the time. Looking back, that was absolutely insane and I can't believe that I allowed that type of controlling behavior.

He used money to control me. That was his sword of power.

Every time I wanted to leave him he would say, *"You won't make it on your own...you can't take care of Amber."*

I believed him because I hadn't yet learned that I am a Divine Goddess with unlimited potential, and that it is my birthright to have all of the riches of the Universe.

CHAPTER 35

"Understand that the right to choose your own path
is a sacred privilege. Use it. Dwell in possibility."
- Oprah Winfrey

Ginger decided to return home to go back to school. She seemed to do well, or so I thought. Her life was hidden from me. I attempted to love her as much as I could each time she came home. Bill got the girls their own cars, which was maybe an act of love, maybe to get them out of the house and away from him, but they both almost killed themselves with those cars.

Ginger, while high on drugs, purposely ran into things in attempts to commit suicide. She finally totaled her car and we did not buy another. She was hardly in our lives, and it was like handing her a loaded gun.

Amber decided to "test" the angels by dodging an 18-wheeler. She ended up totaling her car also, but not under the same circumstances, so her car was replaced. It was replaced again when it was stolen, and then replaced again when it was stolen for the second time. Wow, car thieves love Honda Civics!

Getting Amber through high school and getting her wheels was my unconscious reason to stay in my relationship with Bill. My perception of what I thought was good for my child got fogged by fear; fear of leaving, fear of not being able to make it my own. I gave up years of my life to provide stability to my daughter, when all the while I am sure she would have been happier in a small apartment with a happy mother.

Not soon enough, Ginger flew the nest again, running back to drugs and dysfunctional relationships. Amber was in her senior year of high school and had a car, so it was time for me to break free, but first I had to find a job.

I had a license to practice massage, but I needed a stable income, a salary so I could plan my budget. Massage therapy is great, but you never know what you will make from week to week, and I could not add that additional stress to my life.

The other requirement was to find a job close to Amber's school in a small town with a total of only five dentists. It would take an act of God to find a job that fit all my criteria...and action He took.

My job search was divinely guided by the most random of miracles. I pulled out the yellow pages and began calling the five dentists to see if they were hiring. In small towns people usually keep their jobs for life, so in the back of my mind I thought there was no chance that I would find something. I called the first dental office, the second, the third, the fourth, and found no luck. But on the fifth and final call...

"Hi, this is Aleta. I was wondering if you were hiring for an office manager at this time?"

The receptionist replied, *"Hold on just a second, let me go to another room."*

I was placed on hold, and wondered what the heck that was all about.

The voice returned. *"Do you have experience?"*

I responded, *"Yes I have over fifteen years of experience and ran my husband's dental practice."*

She responded, *"Well, I have been here for ten years as office manager, but I have wanted to pursue my passion and open a restaurant but never felt I could leave the doctor. He has been so good to me, and I have never found anyone with enough experience that I felt I could just turn this place over to."*

And that was it. The act of God. I had my job, I got the salary I wanted, the hours I wanted, and I was set. Next, I had to find an apartment in that small town, which was another challenge. I love small towns, but the apartments are not the prettiest things where most people buy their homes.

I finally found one that someone had just moved out of. It wasn't the best, but it would do. We packed up our stuff, packed up our pain, and set forth on a journey that would be one of the best decisions I have ever made for my children or myself.

Most of my conversation with Bill about me leaving is still blank. I know we discussed separating the stuff, crazy crap that doesn't even matter like certain Christmas ornaments. Really? After fourteen years we're discussing ornaments? I knew it was extremely heart breaking to him, but I was a pro at it. I knew how to shut down my feelings, armor my heart, and move on out.

Run, run, run Aleta.

Without leaving my indifferent marriage, my soul would have slowly melted into the darkness of the life I had created with this man. Deep down he was a wonderful man who did the best he could. In a way, all exes did the best they could. And our parents did the best they could.

The divorce caused financial deterioration for us both. My attempt to get my half of the dental practice turned out to be one of my worst decisions. The more money I gave to the attorneys, the more I went into debt. After charging up all of my credit cards in an attempt to get my half of the practice, I realized that my ex would win because he had the money to keep the fight going and I didn't.

So I gave up for my own sanity. I walked away with a small settlement from our home. I ended up spending that money within a year. I gave guilt money to my daughter for disturbing her life, and I attempted to return to my comfortable financial thermostat, which happened to be on the paycheck-to-paycheck meter.

Oh, what I would do now if I had that to do over again. That lesson was a huge financial jolt for me. I ended up filing for bankruptcy, ruining my credit, and for the first time in years I was driving a ten-year-old car. There is really nothing wrong with that when it's paid for, but it is very wrong when your bad credit causes your finance charges to inflate the ten-year-old car payments to equal the payments of a brand new car.

I hurt him. I hurt him badly. He desperately wanted to save our marriage, but when I'm done, I'm DONE. There was no turning back. Once my heart closed, I wouldn't open it again. The resentments were like mortar, the pain like bricks, and there was nothing that could break that down until I was ready to love again.

He hurt me, we hurt each other, he loved me, and we loved each other. We did the best we could with the knowledge that we had at the time. I attempted to have a friendship with him after the divorce, but he was content with staying angry with me. It suited him, or rather suited his victim-ness. I was one more wife (actually, number six) to add to the list of wives who he could claim screwed him.

CHAPTER 36

"If you don't like something, change it.
If you can't change it, change your attitude."
- Maya Angelou

When the divorce was final, Bill let go of me and he let go of my daughters. I could not understand how a man could raise two children as his own for fourteen years and then just walk away with no conscious. That hurt me, but mostly it hurt my daughter, Amber. I couldn't help but feel that because of my choices in men, she had become the innocent victim of my dysfunction.

Living in our own apartment, Amber and I were setting up our own sacred space. Our freedom was so beautiful and peaceful. Or was it? In truth, it was scary and peaceful at the same time. Joyous, but sad. It was a roller coaster of emotions, ugly cries, snot-filled Kleenex, and moments of, "What do I do with myself now?"

I decided I'd work out, work out all the pain and then eat comfort food. A little contradictory, but at least there was balance in my new life. In truth, I did not know how to live without a man. I had never been without a man in my entire life.

"How does one do this?" I asked myself. *"How do I live alone?"*

After two whole months of asking myself that question, I decided to call Brad, the dentist I had an affair with so many years ago. That would do it. Rather than doing some internal work that could possibly be the key to lasting change and enlightenment, I chose to keep running the same co-dependent patterns that I had my whole life. Yeeaah. That's the ticket.

So off I went into my new relationship with the old lover. I was in the same space at the age of thirty-six as I was seventeen years ago with the same man. He was perfect then. He was a changed, grown man.

He wouldn't cheat on me...he loves me! Right… Did I mention that I knew going into the relationship that he had never been faithful in any relationship in his entire life? That was how much I had deluded myself. That was how strong the pull of co-dependency was for me, and how deeply entrenched that behavior pattern was in my psyche.

All the red flags popped up. His "assistant" called at two o'clock in the morning. She came over to his house and walked in while I was visiting. My gut kept telling me that he was having an affair, and the signs were big, giant billboards with neon lights flashing in front of my face, but I just painted them with a large brush of denial and went on my way with the newfound "love of my life." He whispered sweet everything's in my ear, and I took it in because I needed it. I needed to be treated like a queen. I needed to feel adored, sexy, and spoiled. He did all of that for me. He was really amazing.

Once, he took me to an amazing restaurant.

The waiter came to the table and said, *"Miss Heather, I will get your favorite drink for you."*

I said, *"That's strange. He just called me Heather and brought me a drink that I don't like. Isn't that the name of your assistant? I don't understand."*

When Brad excused himself from the table and the waiter promptly returned with a different drink and called me by my actual name, the paint brush of denial came flying in to do its job again, whitewashing the billboard of AFFAIR that was so obvious and apparent to the rest of the world. I just couldn't let go of the wonderful feeling of bliss I was experiencing, even though he had his fling on the side.

Brad let me pick out a house to buy for "us." We picked out furniture and decorated the house for "us." We spent the weekends together; he brushed my hair every night. We were perfect together, and he made me feel fantastic.

Then things began to get ugly. Like the time he was out of town and I came to check on the dog we bought for "us." All of the pictures of me and of "us" together were broken and thrown in the trash. Then there was the time when I went to visit his family and took a run with his sister. She, in so many words, attempted to tell me that I was unlike anyone her brother had ever been with.

In code she said, *"Run and keep running."*

All of his family kept saying, *"You are the best thing that has ever happened to him."*

But at the same time, they looked at me like I was an alien from another planet. I think what they were really saying was, *"Where did you come from and what has he done with your brain? Do you not see that he is a womanizer?"*

Then I did the unthinkable. I confronted him in a sideways sort of way.

"You know your assistant? I think she is the one who broke the pictures in the house. I want you to fire her."

He assured me he would, and as I returned that night to him sitting in the backyard next to our fire pit, the flames screamed out, *"He is not going to fire her! He is having an affair with her and wants to keep her around, you idiot!"*

"Did you fire her?" I asked.

He looked up at me with a tone of authority and wisdom and said, *"No, I spoke with my attorney and he said that I can't. I have no proof that she broke in, and she can sue me for firing her for no reason."*

I was furious. Fire was coming from the fire pit, as well as my ears, nose, and mouth. That was it, I was going to stomp off and show him, and then he would come after me and make it all go away. At least I hoped he would come find me and love me just as I had always hoped my father would when I was a child. But just like my father, Brad never came either. So I sat in my anger, which then turned to fear and sadness, and I took a shovel, dug a hole, and put my power in it.

I left the next morning for work after doing my normal dance of 'I am so mad at you, please forgive me and hold me' routine.

That afternoon at work, one of my co-workers said, *"You have a delivery in the back."*

I went back to find all of my belongings that I had left at the house we picked for "us" in a duffle bag. That bag was full of shame, regret, pain, slap-in-the-face, you-dumbass, how-could-you-let-this-happen, I-thought-he-loved-me, and it sat in the hall at my place of employment for all to see.

I took it and dragged it to my car in tears, drove to my apartment, and banged my head into the wall while my daughter looked at me as if I had just lost my mind. I had lost my mind along my heart, and my pride.

Had I had enough? Was it over? Oh no, of course not. I would be available to him in any way that I could. I would find a way back into the depths of pain in his arms, someway, somehow. I drove for two hours without knowing if he was home, to "see our dog." I knocked on the glass backdoor looking quite sexy, and asked if I could use the bathroom. As I washed my hands, my heart was pounding, knowing my next step was to force a talk.

"If you wanted to see others, why didn't you just tell me? Be honest. We can date each other and other people if that is what you need. I just want to be with you...I don't want it to end. I know that you felt attacked and pressured by me wanting you to fire Heather, and I am sorry."

And that was it. We were together again, but on his terms, his availability, and his power controlling the strings of my heart. I would just sit and wait for him to call, and when I could see him, I would, and it was so great. I would give him the best sex I could, because that was my power tool. I knew I was the best, and I was going to use whatever I could to keep him in my life.

He told me he wasn't seeing Heather, and I believed him because I wanted to. Our time together was not every weekend, it was very few phone calls and very limited personal contact, but in my mind that was better than being alone. How weak I had become. When I buried my power, I really buried it. I had lost myself in that relationship. I was seeking my happiness and value through another person. If someone liked me and gave me attention, then I was of value, but on my own I felt I was not. That was all I had ever known to be true.

CHAPTER 37

"It's often just enough to be with someone. I don't need to touch them.
Not even talk. A feeling passes between you both. You're not alone."
- Marilyn Monroe

E aster morning, I was shaken out of bed by some higher power that told me, *"Go to his house now. You must drive now. Do not hesitate,* ***go now!"***

"*But I don't want to go,*" I thought. "*I want to go back to sleep. It's two hours away, I don't want to go.*"

"*You must go, and you will* ***go now.***"

So I did. I drove. Someone drove. Angels drove.

I pulled up, knocked on the door, but no one answered.

Then I heard in my head, "*Go to the back door, then go to the bedroom.*"

I went and the door was unlocked. I walked to the bedroom, and everything I had returned to its place from the duffle bag was gone. The pictures of us on the wall were gone. My toiletries were replaced with someone else's. In the trashcan was an empty bottle of Viagra and used feminine cleansing cloths. You guessed it, not mine. And Brad never needed Viagra with me (my ego has to say that).

I looked in the closet, and there on the floor were all of my belongings with our pictures thrown on top. Everything was staring at me in a big pile of, 'No wonder he would never invite you out to the house and wanted to drive to you.'

I looked under the bed and found a treatment plan for Heather to get liposuction, signed by Dr. B. How sweet, he was going to get her fat ass sucked away. How sweet of him. In the nightstand was a picture of Heather and her little girl. How precious.

I was shaking so hard I could not breathe. I did what any woman would do in time of pain. No, not set the house on fire. I grabbed my duffle bag, our pictures, and every single bottle of wine on the wine rack. I headed for the driveway and got in my Jeep to leave. I was abruptly stopped by the next-door neighbor, whom I knew.

She said, *"I thought you two split up."*

I was surprised. *"I guess you and everyone else knew that but me."*

She said, *"He has had so many different women coming and going, I just assumed. He started dating my assistant a couple of months ago and took her to that jeweler in Rockwall to look at engagement rings. He is with her, her family, and his family right now for Easter lunch."*

I was shocked! Not only was Brad seeing someone else, but he took her to the same jeweler he got all my jewelry from. His family knew me, they knew we were together, and they're out with some other woman's family for Easter brunch?

My world came crashing to an end, and Zena the Warrior Princess invaded my body.

"Thank you for this information, I appreciate your honesty."

"No problem. He is a jerk and we hope he moves. I can't believe he treated you like that," She replied.

I turned my jeep around and drove back into the driveway, opened the garage, parked, closed the door, and went in the house.

I hyperventilated, avoided getting drunk before noon, and waited for him and his new family to return home so I could greet them. Oh no you didn't. Oh yes I did! I saw them pull up, him and his new family in his car, while his sister and mother followed in the car behind. He hit the garage door opener and I saw his jaw drop when he saw my jeep parked inside. He briefly spoke to his new lovely, got out of the car, and came into the house.

That man was six foot six and two hundred fifty pounds. I was five foot eight and one hundred twenty five pounds. You can guess that when I talked to him I had to look up.

"Hi honey, how are you? Who's your new friend? Can you introduce me?"

Brad looked like he was about to throw up. *"Just a friend, what are you doing here, babe?"*

"Ummm...well, I was woken up this morning by God and told to come and visit "our" house and you, and I found all of my belongings replaced by another women's stuff. So just exactly how many women are you seeing without letting me know?"

Suddenly, Satan himself was now looking down on me. ("Hi Satan, I've seen you before in my daddy and in my babies' daddy, Wes").

His tongue became a blade as he spewed out the words, *"GET THE FUCK OUT OF MY HOUSE!"*

Wow. That was incredible. Who was that man? I am Zena The Warrior Princess that just turned into Hindu Goddess Kali, and I am not backing down, Satan! I will walk out of this house with power and collect all of my belongings (even though I already had, and they were in my jeep). I will find belongings that I think are mine so I can question you.

"How could you do this?!?"

So, for what seemed like an eternity, I walked the house pretending to search for my belongings, asking over and over, *"How could you do this to me?!?"*

He would repeat, *"GET THE FUCK OUT OF MY HOUSE!"*

After I had made my rounds and got nothing but the same words as an answer to any question I asked, I took my book I found on the shelf and walked to my car. Of course, he ran out there and told them I was a crazy stalker.

I shouted to the woman and her family, *"I am not a stalker. You are going to be hurt. Run while you can, he is seeing many other women. This was "our" house, this was "our" dog, and this was "our" life!"*

Brad told them to call the police because his phone didn't work, which was his way of trying to get them out of there before I could tell her and the family anymore truth. They pulled into the driveway of a neighbor and waited there. I followed them into the driveway (okay, I actually looked like a crazy stalker at that point) and screamed again, *"Please leave while you can! He will crush your heart!"*

I left and drove down the dirt road as the wine bottles clanged together in the back and I listened to the song 'Soak Up The Sun' by Sheryl Crow. I looked in my rearview mirror, and all I could see was dust as I drove away into the sunshine with my duffle bag and my power. I let go of the baggage and kept the power, and I learned to trust my intuition.

CHAPTER 38

"If you have only one smile in you, give it to the people you love."
- Maya Angelou

Soon after my breakup with Brad, I moved myself and Amber into two different homes. Amber got her own apartment a couple of months before she graduated, because the condo I bought was closing before her graduation and I had to move.

I was so excited that I had bought my first home all by myself. It was on Turtle Creek Blvd, one of the nicest parts of Dallas, and even though it was only six hundred square feet, it was mine. It was in a high rise, with granite counter tops and marble floors, and it had a patio that overlooked the pool on the rooftop. I really felt like I was going to begin a whole new life in the city, a new me.

I had never lived alone, by myself, without children or a man. It was a first for me, and I was ready. I wanted to date, I wanted to have lovers, drink wine, go to parties, and reinvent myself. Maybe like Samantha from 'Sex In The City', when really I was more like Carrie. Anyway, the condo was the beginning of the new me.

I was working at another dental office that called itself a 'Dental Spa'. I was looking forward to the job because I would be doing massage again, as well as managing the office. Massage therapy; energy work; cranial sacral were my gifts from The Universe-God. I was a conduit for love and healing, and it was one area in my life that I was confident in. I loved doing bodywork. Healing others through bodywork or through counsel was my true passion.

When I started at the so called 'Dental Spa', I was a little put off when the dentist opened his private office door and started cussing at the receptionist. The receptionist was bitter and had eyebrows that wanted to reach out and grab someone. She scared me. I realized there was nothing 'spa' about the office other than the name.

I attempted to make it work with all my heart because it was located just ten minutes from my new home. When I started coming home in tears because of the way I was treated, I knew that The Universe had another plan for me. I faxed my resume to a dentist in Plano, which was quite the drive, but the position was for an office manager and the salary was negotiable.

The second thing I had become confident in was my skills at any position in the dental industry. With confidence, I knew my value and I wouldn't settle for less. I was offered the job, and I negotiated myself into a sweet salary that made the drive worthwhile.

What I didn't know until after I had been working there for awhile, was that the drama that came from that partnership of two dentists, who hated each other, was not worth any amount of money. Let me just say, I was working with two egomaniacs, who each had pain-body wars on a daily basis.

The doctor who hired me would take me in his office and interrogate me.

"What have you been telling him? What did he ask you?"

It was so ridiculous, but I kept working and making the best of a bad situation. And one day, I received a phone call from a man named Russell, who said that we were one of the dental offices on his insurance plan, and he wanted to come in for an appointment. He was so funny. He had me laughing so hard I had tears running down my face! I ended up talking, flirting, and laughing with him for at least thirty minutes. I have to say, there was something about his voice...the man intrigued me. I wondered if he could be as beautiful as he sounded on the other end of that line. Oh God, what if he looked like an ogre? I had no idea, but we had several flirting exchanges over the phone during the weeks before his actual appointment time. We definitely had a connection! So ogre or prince, I made sure that I looked really hot the day of his appointment.

When Russell entered the front door, my jaw dropped in my lap! He was one of the most beautiful men I had ever laid my eyes on. I knew then and there, it was over. The old movies in my mind of good looking, charismatic men all pointed to one thing: RED FLAG. I could not take my eyes off of his piercing blue eyes. He was tall, had dark hair, a gorgeous body, and when you threw in the laughter factor...oh my. I was swooning.

The dialog in my head was going wild.

"Why would he like me? I am not all that, and if he did like me, then he would surely be a womanizer..."

I just did not need another one of those in my life after my Brad experience. I had had enough of unavailable men.

So as much as I wanted to throw him down in the dental chair and make wild passionate love to him then and there, I was standoffish. He had all the women in the office drooling over him. You could hear them all giggle when he spoke. Boy, was he smooth. He came to the front after finishing with his dental procedure and started chatting with me, letting me know that he was having a kickboxing event that weekend and "we" were all invited.

Oh, that's just great. He was a kick boxer. Could someone please hand me a new pair of panties? Mine seem to be in a state of disarray. I love kickboxers. Then the dialog in my head went wild...

"I love this man. No, I don't. I want him. No, I don't. Everybody wants him. I can't have him. He won't want me. He wants them all. I want him. I have to have him. Oh no, I can't...please leave now!"

I managed to say, *"Thank you for coming in today. I am not sure if I will be available to come to your kick boxing event, but thank you for the invite."*

Pull your tongue back in your mouth. Quickly, before he sees! He left the building, and as I snapped out of it, I realized I forgot to get his money because I could not take my eyes off of him!

I immediately printed a statement requesting the money he owed, and on the statement I wrote, 'Hey big guy, this is what you owe'. Then I walked away from the postal dropbox saying to myself, *"Hey big guy??? Wow, now that was professional. You don't want him at all do you?"*

A couple of days later I get a phone call and he says, *"Big guy??? Is that a term of endearment, or are you venturing a guess?"*

Oh my God, did he really just say that? And how in the hell did he make it sound charming and funny when out of anyone else's mouth it would have been cheesy and lecherous? I was flustered because I had been busted on 'Big guy'.

"I apologize if I offended you—"

"Oh not at all," he said. *"I actually kind of liked it. But let's be honest, we've been flirting since the first phone call. If you want to take me out on a date, just say so."*

I was shocked. I said, *"What?! I'm a lady. I'm not taking you out on a date. You should take me out on a date!"*

To which he calmly replied, *"Okay, deal."*

He got me. *"You totally set me up for that, didn't you?"*

"Yeah, pretty much."

I tried to be as unavailable as I could for as long as I could, because truth be told, I did not trust myself. I knew this man had a hold on me from the moment he said, *"Hi, I'm Russell. I need to make an appointment and I promise not to have garlic for lunch beforehand."*

He finally got me to accept a date by offering to come and make me home made Thai food.

Oh God, you cook too?!?!

I can't deny spicy food or spicy men, and he was the complete package. I think I tried two to three times to cancel the date the day of because I was uncomfortable with him coming to my home, but not because I thought he was going to hurt me. It was because I was going to hurt him, which would then ultimately hurt me.

I already felt a deep connection that man and knew it would not be our first and only date. We were going to be a symphony of emotions, past lives, future lives, parallel universes, time travel, and angelic forces combined together for a lifetime of incredible magnitudes of love.

Wow, no pressure.

After two hours of trying on different outfits (*this one shows too much boob; this one, not enough; this one says I am easy; this one says prude*), I ended up wearing the frumpiest top I could find with pink polka dots.

He knocked on the door and I looked in the mirror and said, *"What was I thinking?!"*

Knock, knock, knock. Oh, the door, get the door! I opened the door and there stood my Greek God with a bag of groceries, dressed all in black, which brought out his eyes and hair even more. He held the piece de resistance: a twenty-pound bag of jasmine rice.

I let him walk in the door, and then stuck my tongue down his throat. Yes, yes I did. I could not help it! It was an amazing kiss, and an amazingly large bag of rice. He explained that the kickboxing instructor who taught him how to cook Thai food always used that brand of rice and he couldn't find it in a smaller bag. He didn't want to risk the meal not being perfect.

We had wine, he cooked, and I just stared at him. He cooks, he kickboxes, he makes me laugh, he is gorgeous, he has a rocking body. What could possibly be wrong with this man? Bad lover? Small penis?

Then he began telling me the life of Russell, how he lived in Israel, then at age seventeen he decided he was going to travel to Scotland and stay in Findhorn (the spiritual community) for a year and go on his spiritual journey.

Ok, that's it, I was in love. He was the man of my dreams. I remember saying to myself, *"This is my Sting, this is my twin flame, this is the man I was destined to spend my life with."*

He left soon after to go to Florida for a one-week kickboxing seminar, and I knew that I must go about my business and let him do the calling. And that is what I did. I could not believe I was able to keep my fingers off that phone. Don't get me wrong, I thought about it. I held back because I just knew that he was one to do the hunting, and I was not going to take that away from him.

I believe it was the second night he was gone that I got a much-unexpected late night phone call from him. He said that he was hanging out with some of the other kickboxers at a bar, and when he got back to the hotel he decided he would give me a call.

Then, in a whisper-like tone, he said, *"I miss you."*

I was blown away! Sure, my first thought was that he was drunk dialing, which he probably was, but my perception of what I thought he might say would be more along the lines of phone sex, not 'I miss you.'

Well, let me just say that it just made my heart sing. I could not believe it. I missed him too, so very much. He was all I could think about and all I wanted in my life was his energy. That man was the man of my dreams, and I knew it to depths of my soul.

He called me again before returning from Florida and said that after a day of sparring and taking a few shots to the mouth, his temporary crown had fallen out that night. He was walking around looking like a toothless thug and was too embarrassed to come and see me when he got off the plane. I assured him that with twenty years of dental experience, I had seen it all and it was not going to bother me. He showed up trying not to smile, and all I could do was embrace him and try not to look and feel too emotional that he was near me.

Shortly after that night I received a blow to my heart. He told me that before we had met, he had an online reunion with his high school sweetheart, and after years without contact they had arranged to meet. She was coming all the way from Israel where they had gone to high school together, and she would be arriving in one week. He said that he had always had an 'I wonder if...' feeling about her, and had thought that she might be "The One," but since he met me he wasn't so sure. He didn't know what to do, but he insisted on being honest with me about it, and I appreciated that more then he would ever know.

I told him, *"You must go spend time with her. You must find what your heart's desire is...her or me."*

He later told me that in that moment he gained so much respect for me and that I tipped the scales in my favor by my decision based in love and freedom rather than fear and control. I was so confident in our love, and I trusted my heart. I knew that telling him that he couldn't go spend time with her was the normal thing that most women would do, but would be the worst thing I could do. If I had done that, then I would have never known if he really would have chosen me. I would have wondered if he would always have it in the back of his head that he might have really made a mistake.

We went to the sauna and did some chanting, sweating, and connecting to spirit. We came back to my apartment, and I sat at his knee and looked up into those beautiful blue eyes and said, *"I finally found you, and I don't know if I can let you go, but you must go to her and find what your heart truly wants."*

It was so hard for me, but it was what I needed to do for both of us. He left and was gone for four days, the longest wait in my life. I did not call him, I let him be, but I sent him my heart energy and continued my inward journey to stay strong and grounded during the time of unknowing.

I was at work when I got the call. He was so excited that I was happy to hear from him, and I did not understand why he thought I would not be.

He said, "I sent you a text message the second night I was with her that said 'I have found my love...and it is you.'"

I had to run out of the office and call him back in the stairwell from my cell phone after looking at the message. I was crying. I didn't receive it when he had sent it. Truth is, at that time I did not know how to receive or read text messages, and he was worried that the feeling was not mutual because I did not respond to him. I could not stop smile-crying! He loved me! My heart had spoken the truth. Never doubt the answers of the heart!

From there we began the most beautiful, painful, incredible, loving, jealous, angry, fabulous, spiritual, growing relationship. What? It wasn't all bliss? Well, of course they all are in the beginning. It's that wonderful honeymoon phase of hormones flooding the brain, each partner appearing to be the perfection that we all hunger for. Don't we all wish that the relationship could stay that way? But that isn't real love at all. It's an infatuation seen through rose-colored glasses that is hormone-driven and all-consuming, before the reality of everyday life seeps in.

My oldest daughter Ginger got pregnant when Russell and I first met. A friend of hers called me at three in the morning and told me that I needed to come and get my grandson, GT (then 3 months old), out of a meth house. Ginger was drugging and was not in her right mind, and GT needed a home.

Russell and I raised him for several months, and then I made one of the hardest decisions ever. I was not in a place to raise him at that time, but I knew he deserved to be adopted by a normal family. I chose the family. It had to be an open adoption so that I could still be Nana.

I was a thirty-eight year old grandmother.

CHAPTER 39

"Love recognizes no barriers. It jumps hurdles, leaps fences,
and penetrates walls to arrive at its destination full of hope."
- Maya Angelou

Russell and I had something else in common from our past...drugs and alcohol. Well, it only took a few fond retellings of old stories to get the endorphins firing, and soon those stories took two people who had been out of the drug scene for many years back into it once again.

Somehow, while re-hashing the past, it reminded us of the great times, but we completely overlooked the hell that comes with that scene. We always felt like shit the next day, mentally, physically, spiritually, and then flogged ourselves for choosing that path. We'd take two weeks to get our heads straight before we started all over again.

That lifestyle breeds jealousy, insecurity, pain, arguments, and poor judgments that leading to more jealousy, and the worst of all, separation from source-Spirit, The Universe, God, the greatness of Life! That separation was the most painful of all, because without that connection to source, you feel alone, ashamed, lost, and you forget who you truly are; divine, a child of God.

We lost ourselves. We lost our self-respect. We lost respect for each other. We lost trust, and we lost what felt like our souls. The pain we experienced during that time was consuming, and the loss of our relationship was the result of those choices. I could no longer feel loved or give love; my heart was closed. My self-respect and my respect for my beloved Russell was no longer present. I don't want to go into all of the different effects or the situations that doing drugs put us in, but I will say that it ruined us inside and out.

Addiction is cunning, baffling, and patient! It would always start the same way, 'Let's go out and have a couple of drinks, we won't use drugs.' Then the drinking starts, and the drugs would follow. Alcohol was always the doorway to drugs for me. When I was sober, I would never say, 'Well, I really would love to go do cocaine tonight.' We didn't even talk about it the next day. We were silent, doing the walk of shame. That went on for two years.

That year I had a birthday trip planned. I was going on a cruise with my Aunt Kathy, Cousin Ryan, and Kerry. It was their birthday present to me. The night before the cruise, I came very close to overdosing. By the grace of God I didn't, and I made it to the ship on time. My family had no idea.

The goal of that trip was for me to conquer my fears. So one of the first things that they had me do when we got on the ship was put on a bikini and go down to the area where everyone in the whole ship had to gather to get safety instructions. Let me paint you a picture...I am the only one in a bikini, wearing a life vest, standing in a group of over two thousand people! I have never been so embarrassed in my life!

Remember, anything that I was afraid of, I was going to do. My family was there to help me get through those fears, but also to razz me like I was a freshman in high school.

I was sick with a fever for the first two nights on the cruise. The fever was my body's response to the drugs I had put in my system three days before. My family wanted me to have fun with them and drink, but I too sick. Thank GOD! I did drink after I started feeling better, but I did not get wasted as I usually set out to do. I was having a fantastic time with my family. It had been a very long time since I had spent time with them, and we had never done any kind of trip like that before.

The next fear I wanted to conquer was karaoke. I know it is fun for some people, but for me it was terrifying! I had been terrified to perform in front of people ever since one specific incident when I was in high school.

I was in a play with one other girl that we were to perform in front of my entire high school class. We had rehearsed for at least three months, or what seemed like a lifetime. I knew my lines, and I was actually a really good actress. I could get into my characters and had so much emotional content to pull from in my life.

On the opening night, the curtains opened, she said her line, I said mine, and then I froze. I literally froze. I could not remember my lines and I could not breathe. I made it off the stage and into the car to be taken home, and I never, ever did theater again.

It is sad that happened, because there is a part of me that has always felt that I could be an incredible actress, because for so many years of my life, I was a character. I was whatever I chose to be in order to not be me.

So now, karaoke it was. I was going to conquer that fear! The setting was not a small bar on the ship; it was auditorium-like with a very large audience. I picked my song, one that seemed simple: 'Hollaback Girl' by Gwen Stefani. The music started and I begin to sing, but I missed some of the lines and could not catch up. I froze again and started crying. I could not move, and to make matters worse, the crowd booed.

Let me just say how much my family rocked at that moment.

My family ran up to the stage, grabbed a mike, and sang with me, while tears continued to pour down my face. But I sang! I cried and I sang. I had so many people come up to me afterwards and say that they were so proud of me. It was then and there that I felt healed by their words and healed by my family.

The cruise was amazing. I needed the love of my family after almost dying the night before the cruise. I shared with them some of what happened, but not the entirety of it. I was too ashamed.

The week I was gone, I had no way of speaking to Russell except for one time when we were in Key West. The connection was bad, and I think we just said that we loved each other. He sent me roses and a teddy bear on the ship, and I could feel him missing me so much. Things were not good between us. We had hit a rough patch that we could not hide from any longer.

When I got home from the trip, Russell was so amazing. He picked me up from the airport and took me to dinner. In the middle of dinner, he got a text message and told me he had to go by the club he worked at on weekends for something when we were done.

So we get to the club and enter through the back door, which was odd, but I didn't question it because I was just so happy to be with him. I walked in and all of my friends and my daughter yelled, *"Surprise, Happy Birthday!"* He had put together a surprise party for me! I could not believe how much he loved me, and that all of those people showed up to honor me. I felt loved!

We went home that night and I just held him, knowing that I was a truly blessed woman. The next day, Russell sat down with me and said,

"Aleta, I can't do this anymore. I have forgotten my glory. I am meant to be so much more than this! I went to AA, and I have been going to meetings. And if that's what it takes to break this behavior cycle, then that's what it takes. You can either join me or not, but I am not going to live like this any longer."

I looked into his eyes and I knew we were done with drugs and alcohol. I was so grateful that he had the courage to do this. I was relieved because I did not know how to make it stop as a couple.

"Of course I will go with you, let's do this together."

We started on our journey to getting clean and sober. It was much harder than I ever thought possible. The time that I had done it ten years earlier for ten years straight was easy. I was just kicking pot, not alcohol, drugs, and the lifestyle of the clubs. I did not realize how caught up in the glitz and glam I was until I was washing clothes on a Saturday night and threw a fit. I did not know what to do with myself. Was I just going to have to suffer and sit there and watch Blockbuster and fold laundry? That was my Saturday night? Oh, this feels sexy! No more getting all dressed up, feeling hot, and dancing and hanging out with all my friends. What was I going to do?

I remember taking myself to a meeting that Saturday night after I threw dirty laundry all over the house in a fit. I sat in that meeting and was just as angry as I could be!

I finally spoke, *"This just sucks! It's Saturday night and I am doing laundry! What the hell am I suppose to do with my life now?"*

All the old timers just laughed, they loved seeing me like that because it reminded them of where they used to be. That is the beautiful thing about the program; you hear exactly what you need to hear, when you need to hear it.

I cried that night, and I cried many more nights that followed. I started getting my Blockbuster and my ice cream or chocolate, and I started to see that the people I thought were friends were nothing of the sort. Once they knew I was not using, they no longer called me or wanted to hang out.

I lost everything, or so I thought. The truth of the matter is, I gained everything. Russell and I continued our meetings, but something happened to us; we drifted apart. We started fighting all the time. Things were not the same. All the resentments we built up during our partying days that had been pushed down and numbed raised their ugly heads. Suddenly, we were not connected any longer. All of our shadows had been brought to the surface and were locked in mortal combat. My jealousy, fear, and insecurity in the red corner, and his ego, fear of commitment, intimacy, and need to be wild and free in the blue corner.

We were so caught up in our pain and resentment that we couldn't see our love and light anymore. We each knew that we were no longer being fulfilled in the relationship. I was so scared. I really felt I was completely alone in a relationship again.

I remember meditating one day, and a voice came to me and said, *"He must leave in order for you to find yourself and your power."*

I ran upstairs and said, *"Baby, you have to move out...you have to leave. We're just hurting each other and we can't continue this any longer."*

We packed his stuff and I walked him to his car, both of us in tears as he drove away. He left a note on the bed for me that said, *"You're not alone. I love you and always will."* I cried the ugly cry, and then I set forth on the journey to finding Aleta, and burying Medea.

CHAPTER 40

"Every time you are tempted to react in the same old way, ask if you want to be a prisoner of the past or a pioneer of the future."
– Deepak Chopra

I won't say the separation was easy. It was the most painful experience that my heart had felt. I loved Russell unlike any other in my entire life. I knew we were meant to be together. He was my beloved, but we had shattered our relationship with drugs and alcohol and we needed to find ourselves clean and sober!

Sleeping without him was the hardest thing of all. I slept with the teddy bear he gave me, and eventually got a body pillow to help with comfort. I missed him so much; it was eating away at me. I was blessed in that I was divinely led to a job at a famous spa that I would not have gotten if I had not been clean and sober, because they drug tested.

I was hired and started training when Russell and I split up, so I dug deep into the new job! I wanted so badly to call him and share with him all of the amazing things that were happening in my life, but I couldn't. We made a deal that we would not speak for a month. He was only supposed to be gone a month, only a month, for us to have time apart and think about what we wanted and then he would come home.

A month went by. I was counting the days, minutes, seconds, but he didn't come home. We sat down to have a talk about it, and he said he didn't want to come home. I was heartbroken. That was not the plan according to Aleta. That was not the plan at all. Russell was having fun being single again. He lived with his friend in an amazing bachelor pad and he didn't want to come home to me!

Well, okay then, I would just dive deep into my work and begin to work on myself. I would do yoga daily and meditate. I would start learning to speak French, and eventually I would date a French Canadian and forget that my heart was broken. I took his pictures down and put them in the closet...and then put them back up. And then the next day I took them down and put them back up again.

He would just be a bachelor. He would just have sex with whomever, and I would just get strong, empowered, find myself, and love myself. I'd get so connected with the Universe that I would fall in love with *me*!

That would show him!

And that is what happened, I did just that. I lay to rest my old self and was born a butterfly. I found out who I was, and I was amazing. I was divine. I was divinity in full form! In all those years of molding myself to be what others wanted me to be in order to keep them in my life, I never knew who my authentic Aleta was. I had no idea what my likes and dislikes were because I always let others decide for me. I had no idea who I was because I became enmeshed and co-dependent in every relationship I had ever been in.

I had become so good at being a puppet for others that I could not figure out how to pull my own strings. I looked in the mirror, and I not only liked what I saw, I was in love. I was in love with me.

My career was better than it had ever been. By taking that job, I tripled my income. I had so much money that I didn't even need to check my account before purchasing anything for myself. I decided I was going to buy myself a birthday present. A trip to Cancun, a spa trip, and I would get a spa treatment every day. It had been one year since the overdose and the trip with my family, one year clean and sober, and one year apart from Russell.

In the meantime, Russell and I had begun talking and hanging out as friends. He stayed with me for about a week when I had a procedure done and took care of me. I noticed that he specifically set up a date while he was staying there and stayed out all night (I think as a test).

But before he went on the date, he came into the room, made sure I was okay, and said, *"This is strange, going on a date with someone else while I am staying with you…"*

While he waited for me to throw a shoe at him or hit him in the face (the old jealous Aleta), I said, *"I know, it is strange. Have a good time."*

He went out the door and I beamed a big smile, because I was not afraid. I told myself that it didn't matter who he dated, there is only one me, and he will never love or be loved by anyone as amazing as me.

Now, let me just tell you that these words would have never come from the old Aleta. She was a scared, beat down, insecure woman, and she had the story to justify that life. Justify yes, I could do that for the rest of my life, or I could take my power back and become the change I wished to see in the world, as Gandhi so beautifully said.

I did begin dating the French-Canadian, and I was very flattered by the way he looked at me. He thought I was the most beautiful thing in the world, and he showed me in both his actions and words. He was a gentleman, had an incredible career, and he went to a great college. He was very good looking and he made me laugh, but he was not my Russell.

I attempted to teach him some of the spiritual lessons that were part of my life, which he was learning and appreciating. He wanted me and that felt amazing, but my heart was still with Russell.

One night Russell came over to use the computer, and he asked if I wanted to go to a movie. I told him I already had a date. He made sad puppy dog eyes that made me want to cancel the date and spend time with him, but I couldn't, and I wouldn't.

I got dressed and then I heard a knock on the door. It was my date. He was supposed to call me before he got there and I was going to meet him outside. But no, he had to come in when Russell was upstairs.

"Awkward, table for one. Awkward, table for one."

My heart was beating. I was so nervous. I put my dress on and walked by Russell and said good night. I went downstairs and opened the door. My date walked in to meet my daughter Ginger and her new little baby Mia, and I thought I would throw up. Ginger had moved in with me to get clean and sober and have her second baby, Mia.

I finally got my date out the door, and as we walked across the parking lot, the strap to my dress broke and my boob almost announced itself. I was so embarrassed. We had to turn around and go back, and I ran into the house to change. Russell giggled at me. He found the whole thing quite amusing.

CHAPTER 41

"Don't try to steer the river."
- Deepak Chopra

Russell and I continued to just do fun things together like rent movies and sit at home on a Saturday night, maybe even throw a load of laundry in while I was at it to top the night off. Yes, I said it...I grew to like staying at home. I enjoyed being free from the nightlife and what went along with it. I did not have very many friends at all anymore, but I never really had them in the first place. I enjoyed my new life.

I was learning that being alone was okay. I really wasn't alone because God was deep inside my heart, and that was the connection that I had been missing all those years. That was the empty hole I was trying to fill with drugs, alcohol, imitation love, sex, and drama. I was very content with my new life, and felt safe and happy and more at peace than I had ever experienced.

Russell and I would work out together, and he began coming over and spending the night with me, or me with him. We did not have sex; we would just hold each other. That went on for six months or so as we grew to love each other unconditionally and with sobriety. It wasn't based on *getting* anything from each other. Not sex, attention, or any of the usual conditions of a relationship. We just made each other's hearts happy again because we were being ourselves and fully accepting of each other as such. We formed a loving friendship that was unlike anything either of us had ever experienced before in our lives, and it was beautiful.

Russell's birthday came, and I could think of nothing better to give him than a trip to Cancun with me for my birthday. But I was still being an empowered woman, and I wanted girl time too. So I decided to split the trip in half. I would spend the first half with my girlfriend, then fly home, grab Russell the next day, and go back!

I surprised him with his ticket at his birthday party! He was so happy, and that filled me with joy. I loved to see him happy. We were there with his family and about one hundred of his friends at a club. We had dinner first, and I sat next to him with his family. His family never divorced me when we split. His mother kept me on track when I wanted to give up; she anchored me when I just couldn't take it anymore. She was my angel.

We danced and had fun without drugs and alcohol. Russell was happy, and he looked so incredibly sexy that I had a very hard time not kissing him. I maintained my space and did not follow him around; I hung out with his mom and sister.

At one point he was dancing with this girl, and let me just say, he can dance. It makes me warm just thinking about how hot he looked. There was a friend of his shooting a video, and people could go and record their own birthday wish to Russell. When I went to do mine, I had such a hard time not crying. All of his friends kept coming up and introducing me to other people as Russell's woman. They did not know we had split up, and I did not correct them. It felt too good.

The woman Russell was dancing with kept following him everywhere. I thought she was his date. She sat down next to Russell's mom and introduced herself and said something like, *"Oh, you're so cute!"* in a very demeaning tone with a pat on her knee. If only you could have seen the look on his mom's face!

It seemed as if she wanted to say, *"Who the #@*! is this bimbo and why is she saying this to me? And if you don't get her out of here I will hit her."*

She never said a word. That look said it all.

Russell saw my discomfort with the situation and grabbed me, took me outside, and said, *"Aleta, I don't even know who she is! I met her once at the club. I've never slept with her and she is not my girlfriend. She keeps following me and acting like were together and I promise we're not."*

I said, *"You don't have to explain anything to me, we're not together."*

I was so confident and had no fear; I could hardly believe that those words were coming out of my mouth. I had changed, I did not fear anymore. And if I did, it was a short time before I would gain control of it.

It did not control me.

He looked shocked, but I could tell something shifted between us that night. I felt his heart open to me, and it was in my hopes and biggest prayers that it would open all the way and never close again.

I went home that night feeling really fantastic. I had fun without drugs and alcohol, and I could see that Russell was looking at me with new eyes.

He sent me a text, *"I know it's late, I just wanted to tell you how much I appreciate your love and support. You mean the world to me."*

My heart sang a song of gratitude! I was so proud of myself. I had not only become the woman I always wanted to be, I had become the woman he always saw in me that I couldn't see.

I still have that text message in my phone. I have all of the ones he sent to me during that time. I would look at them when I needed to connect with him and feel his love. It may sound silly, but it helped to align with his love when I felt we were never going to pull our heads out of our asses.

CHAPTER 42

"If you find it in your heart to care for
somebody else, you will have succeeded."
- Maya Angelou

My birthday trip was approaching fast, but unfortunately before I left, I had another blow to my heart that needed to be resolved. Ginger was using drugs again and baby Mia was only a couple of months old. Ginger was repeating the same pattern that had happened with little baby GT.

So I called the adoptive mom of GT and asked if she wanted a perfect little angel girl, and miracles of all miracles, she did. My granddaughter Mia would be with her older brother and her older adoptive brother in a family that loved them like their own.

I was so hurt that Ginger once again chose drugs over her children, but addiction has no conscience and Ginger had been in pain her entire life. Some mothers keep their children and try to raise them in their active addiction, so really Ginger did the most selfless act of love by letting them go. I was not going to cancel my trip because of Ginger's choices, so I left baby Mia in the care of Russell's sister.

My birthday trip to Cancun started with girl time. Sometimes you just need quality time with your girlfriends to share your ups, downs, and desserts. We enjoyed our spa treatments and I felt rich. I had never been able to buy myself a trip like that before. I paid for it all by myself like a big girl, and I was 40! I was 40 and amazing, I just loved me and I loved my new life.

As much fun as I had with my friend, I could not wait to be with Russell, to let him experience that beautiful paradise. We had a beautiful suite with a hot tub in the middle of the room that overlooked an amazing ocean view. He and I were like little kids at an amusement park.

I was so glad that I choose an all-inclusive resort with meals included, because that man can eat. Wow, can he eat!

On our first night, after eating an amazing meal, he took me out on the deck. It was a perfect night with the moon and the stars and the sound of the waves splashing on the beach. Russell sat me down, pulled a piece of paper out of his pocket, and proceeded to read a really beautiful poem he had written for me. It was deep, and it showed his heart was open. We were in our own private world filled with love all around. We were back together in a real love relationship.

He put a clear crystal heart necklace around my neck and gave me a kiss. It was a wet kiss because of my tears alone!

Russell said, *"You need a plumber because you're leaking."*

It had happened...we made it. We turned it around. We pulled our heads out of our asses and we had found real love. Both of us were very nervous to have sex because we didn't want to mess up the beautiful thing we had created. It had also been about eight months, three days, four hours, and fifty-two seconds. But, who's counting?

So, cautiously, we did it. I would like to say that it was amazing, but it wasn't. It was awkward and okay. We both looked at each other and wondered what was going on. Russell is so good at getting to the core of things, and he just laid it out: we had both spent our life *performing* sexually from our egos, and it did not feel right to do that anymore with each other. We wanted something deeper, something more loving and spiritually connected.

Neither of us really had any idea how to do that, so we just began by not picturing anyone else. We didn't act out with big displays, and we made no sound effects that weren't genuine. We just stayed present with each other, slowed down, stayed in the moment, and saw each other...really saw each other. It took some time, but it became very beautiful once we learned. Not to say that we don't revert back to performing sometimes. It's hard to change old habits, but we were conscious, as we are conscious with all our day-to-day living now.

So that began the rebirth of our love. Our new, real, love relationship began with the willingness to be different than before, rather than doing the same thing over and over and expecting different results. We found ourselves, and in doing so, we opened our hearts to the universal flow of love. We were able to come back together on a different level that filled our hearts with joy, peace, and complete safety.

Our trip ended with a tear on the patio overlooking the ocean as I gave thanks for my new life, my new me, and the new us. Back to Texas we went, as a couple once again. We walked into the house and fell to the ground. We were so tired that we passed out on the floor.

CHAPTER 43

"You are not the drop in the ocean, but the ocean in the drop."
- Deepak Chopra

The journey of our new love had begun. Russell still had his apartment, and we spent time daily watering the garden of our love. We knew that the next step was to move to Los Angeles for Russell's acting career. That was the plan several years ago when we knew that Russell's acting career could only go so far in Texas. There are only so many times that you can hear, *"We would love to cast you for this part, but we are casting out of L.A."* Russell felt he had tapped the market in Dallas, and the next step was to make the big move. We set our intentions, but thought truthfully it would be a couple of more years before doing so. We needed to save money and get all our ducks in a row.

The company I was working for had a spa in L.A., and I was getting so many clients from there that I felt aligned with the universal flow that it was time to move. I had this strong desire to go and ask one of the corporate managers that just happened to be visiting our spa if I could transfer from the spa in Dallas to the one in L.A.

I fully expected her to say, *"Sure in about a year."* But she said, *"You will transfer this September. You are the number one therapist here, they will be glad to have you there to bring their numbers up."*

What?! Oh my God, that was in three months. I could not believe it.

At the same time, Russell was off working on a movie with Billy Zane, and Billy told him not to wait because he had talent and a great look, and he just needed to go for it.

I called Russell to tell him the news, and at the same time he wanted to share with me the news from Billy Zane. I was speaking over him to tell him of my transfer. We could not believe it, we were moving. We were going to Hollywood to fulfill our dreams! The next couple of months were so exciting!

We got my grandbaby Mia safely to her new home out of state. She settled very well with both her biological and adopted brother. Her new family just adored her. She is an angel. I was also was dealing with the heartache of leaving my daughters in Texas. Even though they are both adults, I had never lived far from them. That would take its toll. The beautiful connection that Russell and I now shared helped balance the sadness I was feeling about leaving all my friends, family, and successful job behind.

We began the preparation of moving to another state by first moving Russell out of his apartment and back into our home, the one we shared before we took our time apart. It was so great to have him back home. I had missed his masculine energy and snuggling with him at night. I felt good in my heart once again.

Amber was living with me while she was finishing up college, so we had time to all connect as a family before we moved, which felt great. Ginger had moved back to the drug world after Mia was placed in her new adoptive home. That had been going on since she was twelve years old, so I had numbed myself to her behavior. Looking back, I also feel that I wanted to run to California because I was so done with all of the pain from Ginger's choices, the loss of my grandchildren, and the old life we had lived there. I wanted a new start. I wanted a new life. I had raised my children. It was time for me.

We had a fantastic farewell party, but the party was bittersweet, as my attention was on Amber as I watched her try to drink away the reality of my leaving. Alcohol numbs, but it also exacerbates the problem. I knew what she was doing when I went into the bathroom and she was in the stall with her best friend from sixth grade with her pants down around her ankles.

I asked her, *"What are you doing honey?"*

"I am going to the bathroom," she responded, as she continued to attempt to pull her pants up and sway back and forth, not even grasping her pants.

It was time for us to part. We were driving the moving truck out the next morning, so that was our goodbye. It was the only way Amber thought she could let me go. It was a very sad way to part, but it was how she handled it.

Russell carried Amber to her friend's car as I smiled and cried. Again, it was bitter sweet, not exactly the goodbye I had hoped for. My heart was in such pain to leave her, but deep down I knew Amber needed the separation so she could spread her wings and fly.

And she did just that.

CHAPTER 44

"Life loves to be taken by the lapel and told:
'I'm with you kid. Let's go.'"
- Maya Angelou

The next morning we attempted to start the journey, but my car would not start. Thinking the battery was dead, we called AAA, who came and said nothing was wrong with it. It wasn't until later in the day that we found out it was a bad car key. I had forgotten that the week before I had flushed my car keys down the toilet at a gas station (another one of my Lucy moments) and we had to get new keys made.

Once the key was replaced, we were off. We were so blessed that a friend of Russell's named Jon came up from Houston to help us with the drive to L.A. The drive from Dallas to L.A. is not an easy one, but we were so excited about moving that we thought with the three of us taking turns, we could drive straight through.

Caffeine became a necessity. Between energy drinks, coffee, and those evil little bottles of 7-hour energy, we were flying on the inside, but with a full U-Haul, plus pulling a car on a trailer, driving fast we were not. It was a strange feeling, akin to drinking a case of red bull and then trying to meditate. The two just didn't mix.

We attempted to make it all the way without stopping, but with our delayed start, we just couldn't do it. Suddenly we needed to find a motel, STAT!

We found a cheap motel that looked semi-clean from the outside. We were all so exhausted, we thought all we needed was a bed and we'd be down for the count. I went into the bathroom, and much to my surprise, the black dots on the floor were not dirt...they were cockroaches. I screamed as I ran out of the bathroom and said, *"I don't care how tired I am, there is no way that I can sleep in a room that is already occupied!"*

Russell was half asleep already and confused, but after I explained, he soon discovered that they populated the rest of the room too.

Russell went to the manager and asked for our money back, and then asked, *"How can you rent us a room that's already got a family of twelve in it?"*

The manager returned our money and we were on the road again.

We managed to drive a couple more hours because the roach experience had shocked us awake. We finally found a decent hotel with a clean room, and down we went. If you have ever driven through Texas, you know that it seems to take forever. Texas is HUGE, but we finally got to that beautiful sign that says 'California'!

We found our way to Culver City (a suburb of Los Angeles), where I had pre-booked our hotel prior to leaving Dallas. The only problem was we could not find the hotel. We were looking for a place to turn around when I looked up and recognized a building.

"Russell, this is very strange, but this is the apartment complex that we found and were looking at online in Dallas!"

We loved it when we saw it online, but we thought it would be too expensive. It was so beautiful; it looked like a Zen garden. We really believe in divine guidance, and took note of the fact that L.A. is huge. For us to get lost (ha, ha, universally guided), and to pull up directly in front of the same apartment community we loved was wild. Then, we found out that the hotel I booked was a half a block away on the same street. It was meant to be.

The next day, we began scouring the city for our new home. We thought we could find something less expensive, forgetting that we lived in L.A. and our rent would double. We searched for days, and then just gave in to the fact that we had already found it that first night, but it just seemed too easy. Our guardian angels must have a lot of patience, and I'm sure they probably giggled at us too.

Moving into our home and starting over in a new city that is a world in itself was incredibly jolting. It was overwhelming, but exciting. I started my new job, and being able to transfer was so stress free for me on some levels because I didn't have to learn anything new. But it was really hard on an emotional level.

There was something not right about the way my new co-workers reacted to me. Some people would not even acknowledge me when I greeted them. I could not figure out why everyone there was shunning me. I am an incredibly likeable person. I knew that I didn't smell and I had really fresh breath, so what was going on? I felt like the new kid in school that for whatever reason was not welcomed, when at my old school I was very loved and valued. I was someone that attempted to live her life by the Four Agreements by Don Miguel Ruiz. I really felt like a little hurt girl.

After I had been there for a couple of weeks, someone had the courage to tell me what happened to make everyone treat me like a leper. Apparently, the big wigs from corporate had a meeting with the staff before I transferred. They let them know that I was coming and they needed to step up their game to my level or they would be losing their jobs.

Well, no wonder they didn't like me. I was a threat! I understood why management did it, but I don't think they thought through what it would do to me.

Russell and I were so happy with our new home and new life, but we were not at all prepared for the reality that is Hollywood. The truth of the matter is, we did not have a big enough nest egg before going out there. We were not prepared for the incredible expense that living there would be. Yes, we had our rose-colored glasses on, and thought Russell would come out here and start working immediately on his way to stardom and we would be rich! But that was not the case. We started going into lack consciousness and realized that we had to change our thinking quickly or we were done for.

We remembered that we had heard that Michael Beckwith's spiritual center, Agape, was somewhere in L.A. We had enjoyed him immensely in the movie, 'The Secret,' so we got online and soon became very aware why we were divinely guided to the apartment the night we were lost; his spiritual center was walking distance from our home.

The angels were giggling again.

Walking distance to raising our vibration. Walking distance to not forgetting that we are creators of our world. Walking distance to like-minded people. Walking distance to freedom from lack consciousness. We smiled and knew we were going to be okay. We have been more then okay.

As for Russell becoming an overnight success, well...an actor that wants to succeed and do it fast can't have a full-time nine-to-five job because he can't go to auditions. We both knew before coming out here that my income would have to float us.

In January of 2008, three months after moving to L.A., I decided to take on a second job back in the dental field that was going to double my income. It put me in the situation I told myself I would never enter again...I took the job for the money. Within two weeks of working from 7 a.m. to 9 p.m. and getting one day off a week, my new mantra was, *"I need a break! I can't handle this load any longer."*

I was so tired that I would sleep in-between client's sessions. My body was not happy with that load, nor was my mind. My mantra turned into reality when my subconscious said, *"You want a break? You got one."*

As I said in the beginning of this book, *"I had an accident, or did I?"*

It was raining when I left work, so I walked toward the parking garage to avoid the rain. I slipped on the metal stairs, and both feet went out from under me. I landed hard on the stairs, hit my tailbone, and proceeded to hit every stair in the exact same place until I reached the bottom of the stairs.

I got a break all right. I got a broken tailbone, seven herniated discs, and several pinched nerves. I am a powerful creator. You've heard the saying, 'Be careful what you ask for, you just might get it?' I warn you to be specific, conscious, and intentional in your mantras.

You will get what you ask for, even if you think you are just kidding.

CHAPTER 45

"It isn't until you come to a spiritual understanding of who you are—not necessarily a religious feeling, but deep down, the spirit within—that you can begin to take control."
- Oprah Winfrey

My "break" occurred on January 24, 2008. I didn't go back to work again until 2011. Basically, the entire time we had lived in California I was in pain...mentally, physically, and spiritually. I was not working for the first time in my adult life, and had never had that much time off from "doing." That resulted in the death of my ego, followed by depression, because I had based who I was on what I did. I was a healer, and without helping others, I did not know what my value was.

Not only that, but I am a caretaker, and I could not take care of Russell by "doing" for him. I could not understand my value if I was not doing, I did not know how to just *be*. I became so frightened that Russell would leave me because I was no longer doing.

There was an intense, irrational fear that surged up from my unconscious. It became a learning journey for me. I had to learn to *be*, and to know I was loveable for just being me. So I have been working on being in the moment, living authentically, and knowing that I am okay just as I am. I do not have to be perfect!!

I realized my healing had to include my mind, body, and spirit. The accident forced me to realize that my emotions needed to heal before my back and neck could heal.

When I took on that second job, I was no longer taking care of myself and staying grounded in who I was as a divine spirit. That caused my inner child, who I call Tita (the nickname my grandfather gave me), to rise to the surface feeling abandoned and unloved. Poor little Tita, who had suffered so much in the past, would let me know that she was not happy that I wasn't taking care of her or myself. I think she felt that I had abandoned her when she needed to be loved and taken care of.

I believe our inner child still has much to say to us if we just listen. It is the part of us that loves to play, loves to laugh. When that is ignored or stifled, I believe that part of us will let us know one way or another that it is not happy by way of a little temper tantrum that has to be acknowledged; like falling down a flight of stairs.

Physically, the injuries were extensive. At first I was sent home after they misdiagnosed my injuries, saying I only had a small fracture in my sacrum. They did not do an MRI or a nerve conduction test to fully understand it was much worse than they thought.

I had to find my own doctor to get the correct diagnosis. I laid on my couch in pain for a year before finally having the surgery. It was my belief that I could heal myself holistically, but after a year of mind altering pain and not being able to walk, I caved in and asked for the surgery.

The surgeon repaired my spine by putting six springs in my back. I laughed and said, *"Now I'm a Transformer."* The pain and rehabilitation were intense. The medical staff had me up and walking the day after my surgery. When I returned home, I was determined that I was going to heal no matter how much I hurt. I did a year of painful physical therapy.

During the whole ordeal, Russell was the most supportive, loving man on the planet. He took care of me in every way. Even though my fears of, 'if I don't do anything for him, he will surely leave me' were tremendous, he was my rock. He nurtured and loved me through it.

To this day, I still have back pain, just not to the extent that it was prior to the surgery.

CHAPTER 46

"No one ever told me I was pretty when I was a little girl.
All little girls should be told they're pretty, even if they aren't."
- Marilyn Monroe

On March 16, 2009, I was visiting my grandchildren in Alabama when I got word my Uncle Steve had passed away. He fought a long hard battle with cancer, and graduated to the source of all love and no longer had to suffer.

In my heart, I thought of him as my father because he helped raise me. I took a plane from Alabama to Florida to attend his funeral and connect with my cousins (more like my brother and sister in my heart), and my Aunt Kathy (my heart mother). Even though they divorced years ago, Aunt Kathy had an open enough heart to not only be there to support us, but to be honest about how painful the loss was for her as well. He was her first love.

It was a beautiful sight seeing Steve's wife Lesa and Kathy in the same room, just "being," with no resentments. The service was beautiful. My cousins, Kerry, and especially Ryan, did an amazing job of honoring our father with a wonderful service. Because Steve had left no instructions as to his wishes for his funeral, Ryan just honored him in the best way he knew how. Ryan truly stepped up to the plate when he was under so much emotional stress from losing his father. I was so thankful.

The Universe helped with everything, including providing a wonderful sacred space for us all to gather that faced the ocean, which Steve loved.

As I previously mentioned, I have always had a tremendous fear of public speaking, and when asked to speak a bible verse for the service, I almost said no. But I thought about it, and if there was anyone in this world that I would walk through that fear for, it was my Uncle Steve. It took all I had not to pass out, and my heart was pounding as fast as a galloping horse, but I did it for my Uncle Steve.

As I got up in front of everyone, I said, *"I have a huge fear of public speaking, but this is to honor my uncle who was a father to me. I love you, Uncle Steve."*

I made it through just fine. I imagined it was just me and him up there talking. I could feel him standing beside me, listening, and he was proud of me for walking through my fear.

After the beautiful service and just as the sun was beginning to set, we all went out on the patio together. As the sun dipped into the water, we said goodbye to the body, not the spirit, of Steve.

We simply said, *"And so it is..."*

It was truly beautiful. I will love my uncle forever, just as I do my grandpa. They are my angels now.

The loss of Steve brought up a lot of feelings beyond the standard feelings of loss of contact with a loved one. For our family, it was something much different. He was the last of our blood elders. Our Grandpa Ken (Steve's father) passed when he was only fifty-two. Our Grandma Lee was only in her early sixties, and my father was only thirty-four. Our family didn't create longevity.

That realization hit me hard; how life should not be taken for granted. Every day is truly a blessing. I was only forty-four at the time, but for the first time in my life I started thinking about my death and how much more I wanted to do and be. How important it was for me to get this story out to people to help them heal before I leave this body. It became my ultimate goal.

I felt that as far as loving and being loved, I really had been blessed with both. I felt that my spiritual connection was beautiful and that my relationships were also very beautiful. I know that I have loved with an open heart, and will continue to do so. I have no regrets in that department of my life.

So as I went through the loss of my last elder male relative, I realized I have a desire deep inside me that I want to give more to the world, to make a difference with this book and to really help guide people to their best life. Love is what life is really all about. For that I know if I graduate tomorrow (the gift of death, going home to source), *"I did good, I did real good!!!"*

CHAPTER 47

"Many of life's failures are people who did not realize
how close they were to success when they gave up."
- Thomas A. Edison

My Story will never end...for as long as I am alive the story continues, but it does not define me. The lessons I learned from each chapter in this book, each lesson in my life, are based on forgiveness, compassion, love, and the power of grace from God, The Universe, or whatever you choose to call all love, no matter the situation. I truly see now that my parents were just damaged children that grew into adults who chose to use alcohol and drugs to numb their pain. The pain and torture that they gave me was only a reflection of the pain and torture within their hearts. I will never truly get to the bottom of what happened to my father and mother as children, that will be a family secret that will never be revealed, for those that know have passed to the other side. I truly have complete forgiveness and compassion for them, and know that they did the best that they could. They did not possess the ability to see the light that truly was inside of them all along because they were blinded by the fog of addiction and pain of the past.

I have deep love and compassion for my four long-term relationships, each lasting fourteen years, nine years, fourteen years, and nine years, respectively. That seems very strange when I put it on paper, but it is just another part of the puzzle that is my life, which all lead to the place of pure light: my life as it is now at age 47.

Fourteen years with my father: he gave me life, he gave me pain, and he loved me with all his heart, the heart that was closed and toxic. What I learned from him was how to love in spite of not being loved. I learned how to be soft and hug, for I was not hugged. I learned that my father beating me, mentally attempting to break my soul, was not enough to take away my spirit and my faith in something bigger, something better. I ultimately learned that there is nothing that anyone can do to me that can't be changed with the radical action of faith and forgiveness.

The nine-year on-and-off relationship with my daughter's father: he gave me love, he gave me pain, he gave me my beautiful daughters, and he did the best he could despite his past. He was abandoned and abused and had an alcoholic father. I learned that miracles happen (my daughters) even in the midst of insanity. I learned that giving birth at fourteen and in complete fear changed my daughter's ability to feel safe upon entering this world. I had to forgive myself.

"If you know better, you do better." - Maya Angelou

I learned I deserved better than the choice I made in him, for he was my father all over again. I learned that no one has the right to physically or mentally abuse me. I learned that my value was more then a punching bag, and that I deserved something better. I learned that your children witnessing your abuse changes them to the core, and will forever haunt them until they realize that it was not their fault and attain forgiveness.

Fourteen years with my ex-husband Bill: he loved me, he supported me, and he truly gave me all he could give. His mother was not kind to him as a child, and she made him feel less than a man. After his parents divorced, his mother was bitter and angry for years, and he mimicked that behavior. He was married five times before me, all attempts to heal the wounds of the past. He isolated himself and his heart from being able to give and receive love. Bill gave my daughters and me the love that he could give, and he helped me raise my daughters in a beautiful home and a quality of life that I could not have given them at the time. For that I will always be grateful.

I learned that you can be alone with someone sitting right next to you. I learned that if there are signs in the beginning that tell you a person has intimacy issues, that you can't fix them and to move as fast as you can from that relationship. I learned that sometimes relationships just don't last. It wasn't a failure; people really do "grow apart." I was twenty-one and he was seventeen years older than me when we met. Of course I was going to grow into a woman. I learned that I wish I had not married when I knew it wasn't right in the first place. I wish I had saved marriage for THE ONE—the one meaning the one God chose for me that started with an excellent foundation, stability in the mind, and an open heart.

My one-year-on—fifteen-years-off—one-year-on (and to this day friends) relationship with Brad: I am grateful that he showed me how I deserved to be treated—when he wasn't repeating patterns from his past, i.e. cheating. He really treated me like a queen. I learned that I was smart from the beginning of our relationship, and that I could associate myself with people of a higher education, even if I didn't have one. I learned my value as a person and as a woman from that relationship, both from the amazing ways he treated me and the painful ways he hurt me. I learned to trust my intuition and to not create a story that someone will change because I was different then the others. It didn't matter if I was different than the others he hurt in the past, what mattered was what was within his paradigm of thinking that was based on his past. I believe he shared with me that his father also cheated, and was married several times. I am not God. I can't change anyone's thought process. But I can be an example to others, and they can change their own mind. We do not have the power to change anyone on this planet but ourselves.

My nine-year relationship with Russell: I will say only this, I am in complete gratitude for the journey, and the story of this relationship will be continued in my next book.

As far as my relationship with my birth mother, I learned that the one person in your life that is to love, but does not know how to give you love, changes your being. I learned that to this day I still have a challenging time trusting women. I have grown in this area, but still have times when I have to realize I am protecting myself from a woman that has not been in my life for years, which should not affect my attempt at a relationship with a woman in the present. I learned to be a loving mother, maybe not when I was younger, but now. I learned that women hold pain and abuse in, for they feel guilt and shame from the predator. Also, predators can be women, even though they are mostly categorized as men. I learned to trust in my only mother—mother earth—nature, rainbows, cotton candy, and unicorns, ha ha. I learned that if you do not have a mother guiding you to become a woman and are left to the wolves, it takes many years to define your value and who you really are. You have to raise yourself into the woman you read about in spiritual books—women like Oprah Winfrey, Maya Angelou, Mother Theresa, and women like me, normal women who have overcome obstacles that destroys others. I had to find the value in what I had overcome and the strength it took to rise above my past before I could step into the light, step into my glory as a strong, beautiful, empowered woman filled with light, love, and joy.

So, in closing, I am going to share this conversation I had with my daughter Ginger:

Ginger, my oldest daughter, called and said she loved me and needed me, and then began to tell me that last week she had so many needles in her arms and that it felt too good. She knows that this could take her down. I felt this deep knowing as I spoke to her, and told her that if she went back out that I would not have a daughter anymore, she would die. She really will die, and I won't have my beautiful Ginger...not the drug addicted one, but the beautiful soul that has been lost to me for many years. My daughter, my beautiful daughter, is an addict. I can't help her. I can't do anything but love her as I always have, unconditionally. I can only hope and pray that she will see herself as the light she truly is, that she will see that she is not her story.

I will end with this pivotal moment in my life, the thought of losing my beautiful daughter Ginger to drug addiction and knowing that She Is Not Her Story. I truly trust that even if she dies, that she will return to the source of all love. This is what I wish for her, peace in whatever form that takes. I would rather her die and be at peace, than to live in a created hell of addiction and shame.

I look at this story of my life and my daughter's story, and I think of the amazing ability that God gives us to choose, to choose the path that will bring us back home. What will you choose? What will your glory be? Will you allow your light to shine and go forward into the clarity of who you truly are?

Or will you open up to the glory of knowing that you have never left the source of all that is? Will you finally see who you really are behind the mask of ego that tells you that you are not good enough? Is there something inside you that lets you know that where you're heading is not where you should be going at all? As if you're G.P.S. (God Positioning System) has been completely cut off by you?

Just listen to your inner self. It's all inside of you. Just listen.

If you feel good, then you're on the right path. Look around and see if you are not accepting your greatness. What are you so afraid of? What is it that keeps you so stuck? When will you step into the truth of who you really are? When? Is now a good time? Fire the Liar!

My dear friend, my dear loving soul, you are beyond good enough! There is only one YOU, and you are perfect! You are a light that shines bright for the whole world to see!

You, my dear child of God, are ***not*** your story!

I love you.
Peace, love, and light,

Earth Angel Aleta

EPILOGUE

Beautiful one, I thank you for taking the time to read my story. It has been my dream to help others through my story for over twenty years, when Oprah inspired me. The fact that you are reading this means my dream has come true! My wish is for The Story and The Glory (my next book) to bring you to a place of knowing how loved and valued you are on this planet.

During the recovery time after my injury, I started doing freeform writing. I just let the words flow freely through me and onto the paper. Here are some of my favorite pieces. They were written during my transition from ego. I feel that your higher self knows what I am saying, even if your ego tells you differently. Fire the Liar. The ego is not your guide unless you let it be. Here are some of my favorite pieces:

Could there be any stronger feeling or vibration than Love? It is the source of all that we seek to complete us. The emptiness that we try and fulfill with drugs, food, sex, and work all lead us back to the source of our emptiness, a lack of connection with source, the source of ALL LOVE. Love is God-The Universe (or Buddha, or whomever you choose to call a higher source), a non-judging energy, all-encompassing beauty that resonates within our soul on the deepest level. Like plugging into an energy source that replenishes our body, mind, and spirit. When we fall in love, when we look into the eyes of this person, we feel complete. What we see in the depth of the eyes, which is the portal to the soul, is ultimately God. God is in all of us, we are one, we are divinity. What scares us most is our own divine nature and power. One energy, one force. We are not separate; we are all connected. So when you hurt another, you hurt yourself. Loving yourself is loving the world! Peace, joy, happiness, love, all high vibration resonates across the world like an angel's breath on the ocean, sending a wave with that breath. Your attitude, your energy, affects the world in a negative or positive way. You are a force of one, which is never separate from the whole, so the one is the whole. Once you truly accept your power and your own divinity, what will you do with that power to help the world? Will you hoard it for yourself, or will you send your song out to the Universe filled with love and peace?

I hope you enjoyed some of my freeform writing, it shows a glimpse of my glory.

Next Two Books to Follow:

"I Am Glory (A Guide To Healing Your Mind, Body, And Spirit)"

In my next book, *"I Am Glory,"* I will go into detail about all of the empowering tools I used, including meditation, exercise, cleansings, non-traditional healing modalities, and even anti-aging secrets that were all part of my journey. *"I Am Glory"* will give you the tools to help you step out of Your Story and into Your Glory.

"I Am Not Crazy (My Spirit Is Just Crying)"

This book is the continuation of my journey since *"I Am Not My Story."* I will tell you about my discovery that I have P.T.S.D., where my relationship with Russell has led me, my struggle dealing with the pain from my back injury, updates on my daughter Ginger's journey, updates on my daughter Amber and the life-threatening struggles with her son's health, and I will share all the beautiful miracles that have happened in the second half of my life.

Made in the USA
Middletown, DE
31 December 2020

28272047R10104